Taíno Mythology

An Enthralling Guide to the Myths, Legends, and Folklore of the Taínos

© Copyright 2025 - All rights reserved.

The content contained within this book may not be reproduced, duplicated, or transmitted without direct written permission from the author or the publisher.

Under no circumstances will any blame or legal responsibility be held against the publisher, or author, for any damages, reparation, or monetary loss due to the information contained within this book, either directly or indirectly.

Legal Notice:

This book is copyright protected. It is only for personal use. You cannot amend, distribute, sell, use, quote, or paraphrase any part, or the content within this book, without the consent of the author or publisher.

Disclaimer Notice:

Please note the information contained within this document is for educational and entertainment purposes only. All effort has been executed to present accurate, up-to-date, reliable, and complete information. No warranties of any kind are declared or implied. Readers acknowledge that the author is not engaging in the rendering of legal, financial, medical, or professional advice. The content within this book has been derived from various sources. Please consult a licensed professional before attempting any techniques outlined in this book.

By reading this document, the reader agrees that under no circumstances is the author responsible for any losses, direct or indirect, that are incurred as a result of the use of the information contained within this document, including, but not limited to, errors, omissions, or inaccuracies.

Free limited time bonus

Stop for a moment. We have a free bonus set up for you. The problem is this: we forget 90% of everything that we read after 7 days. Crazy fact, right? Here's the solution: we've created a printable, 1-page pdf summary for this book that you're reading now. All you have to do to get your free pdf summary is to go to the following website:
https://livetolearn.lpages.co/enthrallinghistory/

Or, Scan the QR code!

Table of Contents

INTRODUCTION 1
CHAPTER 1: BEGINNINGS: THE CREATION MYTH OF THE TAÍNO PEOPLE 3
CHAPTER 2: GODS AND GODDESSES: TAÍNO ENTITIES 16
CHAPTER 3: ANIMAL SPIRITS AND THEIR ROLE IN TAÍNO MYTH 25
CHAPTER 4: COHOBA RITUALS AND SACRED CEREMONIES 55
CHAPTER 5: THE CEMÍS: SYMBOLS AND IDOLS IN TAÍNO CULTURE 60
CHAPTER 6: THE MYTH OF GUABANCEX: THE TAÍNO STORM GODDESS 65
CHAPTER 7: LIFE, DEATH, AND AFTERLIFE: TAÍNO BELIEFS AND LEGENDS 71
CHAPTER 8: BATEY: THE BALL GAME AND ITS MYTHOLOGICAL SIGNIFICANCE 77
CHAPTER 9: THE ENDURING LEGACY OF TAÍNO MYTHOLOGY 80
CONCLUSION 88
GLOSSARY 90
HERE'S ANOTHER BOOK BY ENTHRALLING HISTORY THAT YOU MIGHT LIKE 93
FREE LIMITED TIME BONUS 94
BIBLIOGRAPHY 95
IMAGE SOURCES 101

Introduction

The day of October 12th, 1492, was life-altering for an entire culture. This was the day Christopher Columbus first met with the Taíno people on the Antillean Islands. From this point on, the vibrant Taíno culture became oppressed by the Spanish. They were subjected to enslavement, starvation, and forced labor. Many perished due to the plagues and viruses that came with their oppressors. Slowly, their culture disappeared as the Spanish language and culture replaced the Indigenous way of life.

But did it actually disappear? For a long time, experts claimed that the Taíno had been driven to extinction, but a closer look indicates something very different. Spanish may be the language spoken in Puerto Rico today, yet if you look closely, there are traces of the Taíno culture and DNA all over Puerto Rico and the surrounding islands.

Today, we generally consider the Taíno origin story and their pantheon of gods and goddesses as myths, though there are descendants today who are working diligently to preserve the religious stories and language of the Taíno. Many modern Taíno are keen to return to their *Primera Raiz*—that is to say, the primary root of their heritage.

When reading about Taíno myths in this book, it is important to consider the full picture of each myth rather than view each tiny detail separately. A myth should be studied like a beautiful painting. Instead of focusing on each single brush stroke, each separate color, and each texture alone, it's best to step back and take in the entire picture as a whole, admiring how each of the overlapping elements comes together into a full image that portrays emotion and evokes questions from the viewer.

Myths can be thought of in this same manner. Just like a painting will give each individual person different feelings and can be interpreted in multiple ways, so can a myth. The ancient ones who gathered these myths into stories had a vastly different worldview than what we have today, which is important to remember while enjoying and interpreting these stories, along with the alternative versions offered.

Myths have the unique ability to blend reality, truth, symbolism, and storytelling into a compelling story. The simple fact that these ancient myths were preserved and still continue to be passed down between generations hundreds or even thousands of years later speaks to their enduring relevance and importance, even in the present day.

With this in mind, we invite you to dive straight into this book. Get ready to enjoy the vivid and complex world of the Taíno people!

Chapter 1: Beginnings: The Creation Myth of the Taíno People

Who Were the Taíno People?

We know that the Taíno were a part of the Arawak nation, the Indigenous people of the Antillean Islands and South America. Some of the Arawak also traveled to Florida, where they divided into several tribes. They landed there around 400 BCE.

The Taíno inhabited what is present-day Puerto Rico and other areas of the Caribbean, sharing their gods and goddesses with the related tribes who inhabited the nearby islands of Haiti, the Dominican Republic, Jamaica, and the Bahamas. The Taíno believed that the gods primarily inhabited one side of the island while the humans inhabited the other side. In fact, in their creation tale, the first humans actually came out of caves on the island of Hispaniola, present-day Haiti; meanwhile, the gods inhabited the other side of the island, the present-day Dominican Republic.

Before we discuss the colorful creation stories and beliefs of the Taíno people, it will be helpful to have an idea of who they were and what type of life they lived.

Taíno: Daily Life

The Taíno people lived in sturdy huts constructed from materials on the islands. These homes were called *bohios*. Their circular huts were strong enough to withstand most hurricane-force winds. Their chiefdoms were called *cacicazgos*, and they were led by a tribal chieftain known as a *cacique*. The leaders were not only males; females could also be the head of a chiefdom. The stories of two Taíno queens are explored further in Chapter 10.

The caciques traditionally lived in a rectangle-shaped hut to distinguish them from the others. The Taíno ancestral tradition was matrilineal, which means they passed down their ancestry through the female side of the family.

Each village included priests or medicine men called *behiques*. Below the ruling class, there was another class of people who were considered secondary nobility. This class was made up of trained warriors called *nitaínos*. The lowest class of people was the general working class called the *naborias*.

When Christopher Columbus "discovered" the Taíno people of Hispaniola, there were five kingdoms or chiefdoms. Each kingdom had dozens of villages full of Taínos. They lived very busy lives, primarily growing fruits and vegetables for nourishment with sophisticated agriculture techniques to avoid devastation from storms and animals, such as the hutia, a large rodent.

The Taíno also hunted and fished, utilizing all of their abundant natural resources. They traded the resources found on their islands with other kingdoms, possibly including the Aztecs and the Maya. The Taíno had a busy maritime trade, with boats constantly sailing throughout the Caribbean and possibly to and from Central and South America. These dugout canoes were loaded with goods, including cassava, fish, and cotton.[1]

The Spaniards had never come in contact with any Indigenous American people before stumbling upon the Taíno. They viewed the Taíno as less civilized than themselves, primarily due to the Taíno people's lack of clothing and more rustic way of life. They were also generous, which Columbus himself noted and considered naive.

---

[1] "Taíno Society." *Historical Archaeology*, www.floridamuseum.ufl.edu/histarch/research/haiti/en-bas-saline/Taíno-society/. Accessed 15 Mar. 2024.

In Taíno society, men wore only breechcloths or loincloths, while women wore dresses or aprons made of palm fibers or cotton. They wore gold necklaces, earrings, and nose rings on special occasions and decoratively painted themselves. As it was hot in the Caribbean region, they had no need for the heavy clothing worn by the Europeans, and they weren't concerned about nudity. The Taíno slept in hammocks in their huts, and they were happy hunting and swimming in the beautiful Caribbean.

Contrary to the Spaniards' belief, the Taíno were not uncivilized. In addition to a busy economy and cultural trade, they also had a well-developed and stable political system. They enjoyed poetry and music, and they played a ball game called *batey*, which used a rubber ball.

The Arawak language has been traced back to 400 BCE, first emerging in South America. The language evolved over time, splitting into many dialects based on region and tribe. In the Caribbean region, the arrival of Columbus and the enslavement of the Taíno people erased much of the Taíno language, instead replacing it with Spanish.

Today, we can find hints of original Taíno words still spoken across the region. These words have entwined themselves in the Spanish and English languages. You are probably familiar with some of them. For example, the word "hurricane" comes from the Taíno word *huracán*. The iguana is a Caribbean lizard and a Taíno word. "Hammock" comes from the Indigenous word *hamaka*. The Taíno people ate spiced roasted meat called *barbacoa*, which has evolved into our English word "barbecue."

By the year 1550, the Taíno population had been decimated. Due to the actions of the Spanish invaders, at least seven million Taíno people died from a combination of disease, starvation, and slavery. One estimate is that at least one-third of the Taíno died from smallpox, which the Spanish introduced to the Native population.[2] The enslaved Taíno were worked to death on plantations or in mines under the watchful eye of men who weren't afraid to inflict brutal violence on them.[3] Starvation killed still more Taíno people, as the plantations and mines disturbed

---

[2] Who Were The Taíno, The Original Inhabitants of Colubus's Island Colonies? - Smithsonian Magazine Article - https://www.smithsonianmag.com/history/who-were-Taíno-original-inhabitants-columbus-island-73824867/

[3] "Tribes - Native Voices." *U.S. National Library of Medicine*, National Institutes of Health, www.nlm.nih.gov/nativevoices/timeline/170.html#:~:text=Christopher%20Columbus%2C%20who%20needs%20to,culture%20on%20Hispaniola%20is%20gone. Accessed 15 Mar. 2024.

the delicate ecosystem, and certain areas became overfished. Many unique marine animals, birds, reptiles, and plants that had once been abundant food sources became nearly extinct, while others went entirely extinct, such as the Alco dog, which was kept by the Taíno as a pet and did not bark.[4]

Bird figure made by the Taíno.[i]

In 1998, the Taíno culture made headlines when descendants from the Dominican Republic, Puerto Rico, and other neighboring regions came together to form the United Confederation of Taíno People. The

---

[4] "Webster's Dictionary 1828 - Alco." *Websters Dictionary 1828*, webstersdictionary1828.com/Dictionary/alco. Accessed 15 Mar. 2024.

goal of the federation is to give a voice to the ancestors of the Taíno and to make an effort to stop the complete loss of their culture and language.

Though the enslavement and abuse by Spaniards and the spread of European disease destroyed most of the Taíno culture in the late 1400s and early 1500s, the Taíno influence, beliefs, and traditions remain strong in the Caribbean island cultures today. Their creation myth and religious beliefs are still well known and practiced in various forms throughout the Antillean Islands.

The Taíno creation myth is a complex story, and it forms the central part of Taíno spirituality. There are, of course, several variations to the story. The Taíno people had no written language. They shared their origin stories by word of mouth, leading to slight changes in details between tribes and time periods.

The first person to write down these creation stories and other information about the Taíno gods and goddesses (also known as *cemís* or *zemis*) was a man named Ramón Pané. Pané was a Spaniard who arrived at the Antillean Islands with Christopher Columbus on his second voyage in 1494. He was a young friar who was assigned to live among the Taíno and learn their language. Columbus requested that he write down everything he could gather about the Taíno culture. A lot of our current knowledge of the Taíno culture comes from Pané's writings, though there was much he didn't understand about their customs.

The English translation of the title of Pané's resulting book is *Relation about the antiquities of the Indians which, with diligence, as a man who knows their language, he has collected by order of the Admiral.*

Taíno Creation Story

In the beginning of time, everything was dark and quiet, almost as if everyone was asleep. Atabey, the mother goddess, was ever-present. She had existed forever. There is no record of her creation or birth. Atabey felt as if something important was missing, so she harvested magical elements from around her and created two children. She named them Yúcahu and Guacar.

Yúcahu noticed that their universe was missing light. Everything was still sleeping, and there was no life anywhere. Atabey was pleased to hear of this observation because she knew it meant that her son Yúcahu could finish the creation she had begun.

First, Yúcahu formed the hot, glowing, burning mass that is the sun. This gave light and heat to Earth. Next, he reached down to Earth and collected precious jewels and stones from its depths. Those he left strewn across the sky as brightly shining stars to help light up the moon, which he had also formed.

Yúcahu gave life to Boinayel, the god of the sun, and Maroya, the goddess of the moon. The warmth and light from the sun made the ground fertile. Trees began to sprout and tower over the planet. Many lush, green plants grew, covering the surface of the land.

Then, Yúcahu decided to create birds to fly in the sky and live among the trees and animals to live among the plants. After a while, he decided there was *still* something missing. This was when he got the idea to create something that was more than an animal but not as powerful as a god.

Yúcahu created a hole in the heavens, and from it sprang the first soul: a human man he named Locuo. Locuo enjoyed the beautiful earth that Yúcahu had created. The plants provided endless food, the trees gave shelter, and the sun gave him warmth and happiness. The land was beautiful in Locuo's eyes. He bent down to worship and gave Yúcahu all of his thanks and praise for the lovely planet.

However, all was not to remain happy and good. Guacar was watching his brother, Yúcahu, and the newly created man, Locuo. Without saying a word, he ran away to a very secluded place and pouted, as he was overcome with jealousy and envy. As he sat and stewed in his unhappiness, some say he decided to change his name to Juracán, which is very similar to the Taíno word for hurricane.

All of the jealousy and rage swirling inside of Juracán changed him from a pleasant god to a terrifying god of evil and destruction. Juracán brought strong winds upon the beautiful earth that Yúcahu had created. From time to time, the winds were so strong that they would destroy an entire area. The towering trees toppled to the ground, flooding rains blew across the land, and plants and animals were killed in the bluster.

Locuo's lovely world turned into a place of anxiety and fear. He could not predict when the terrible winds and deluges of rain would come to his paradise and wreak havoc.

Juracán thought of a new game. He sent indescribable tremors, shaking and rolling the entire world and further traumatizing poor Locuo. One day, Juracán created such a powerful earthquake that the land split into two pieces, sending parts of Earth's crust floating away into the sea. This was the moment the Antilles were formed, becoming the chain of islands containing present-day Puerto Rico.

During this time, Locuo was just trying to survive. Yúcahu decided that Locuo needed other gods to assist him in his struggle to live through Juracán's wild and devastating games. Yúcahu taught Locuo to make images of the gods. These images were named cemís.

Life slowly improved again for Locuo. Yúcahu gave him the gift of fire, teaching him how to cook delicious food and giving him the power of light and warmth on dark nights. Locuo once again became content, enjoying his life on the gorgeous planet.

Sometime later, as Locuo was lying down, deeply appreciating the beauty around him, he reached down and pulled his belly button wide open. Out came two humans who looked similar to him. One was a man, and the other was a woman. The man's name was Guaguyona. The woman was named Yaya, though in some versions, Yaya is also referred to as a man. His two descendants populated the earth with more humans. Sadly, the humans continued to be tortured by Juracán. He plagued the land with deadly winds and wild floods.

Juracán also added a new element to his game. He sent down evil spirits to wreak havoc among the humans living on earth. These evil spirits destroyed the canoes the people used to travel through the water. They rained stones upon the people's homes, destroying the roofs and harming the people inside. When the people were playing their favorite sport, *batey*, the evil spirits would take the ball and hide it. When the people were living happily, the evil spirits would plague them with illness and disease.

Using Yúcahu and Juracán, the Taíno people explained the beginnings of good and evil. They applied these ideals to other people who arrived on the island of Puerto Rico, calling the fierce warring tribe of Caribs, who they believed were sent by Juracán from the islands to the southeast of Puerto Rico, evil. The Taíno also mistakenly thought the arrival of the Spaniards, including Christopher Columbus, were good people sent by Yúcahu. Instead, the Spaniards' establishment in the area only led to their suffering and downfall.

The Taíno have another creation story explaining how the ocean and the fishes of the sea were created. The people of Puerto Rico live on an island where seafood is a key part of their diet. The ocean was essential to the survival of the Taíno, so it's only natural they would have a tale to explain the creation of the waters and the sea life within it.

The Ocean

The story of the creation of the oceans falls somewhere in the middle of the drama between Yúcahu and Juracán. It goes like this.

A spirit, sometimes referred to as Yaya (perhaps a version of the Yaya mentioned in the previous creation myth), fathered a son named Yayael, meaning son of Yaya.

Yayael was upset and wanted to murder his father. Upon discovering his son's deadly plan, Yaya sent him away to calm down. He was banished for four months. When he was allowed to come back, Yayael was still angry. Though it was a difficult decision, Yaya could see that Yayael was a threat to his life, leaving Yaya with no choice but to kill his son. Yaya placed the bones of his son in a gourd and hung it up from a rafter in his house.

After a very long time had passed, Yaya started to feel sad and wanted to look at his son again. He and his wife (whose identity is never revealed) took the gourd down and saw that their son's bones had become fish. Yaya and his wife decided to cook and eat some of the fish, and for the first time, the smell of cooked seafood reached the noses of the gods and spirits.

This was not to be the last of the gourd containing Yaya's son's remains, however.

The Quadruplets

Some years later, Atabey incarnated into a human form. She became the mother goddess, Itiba Cahubaba. During her time as the mother goddess, she gave birth to a set of quadruplets.

The four babies had been cut from the abdomen of the dying woman, resulting in a bloody birth that was seen as a sacrifice for the sake of the Taíno people. After her death, the spirit of Atabey left the body of Itiba Cahubaba, where she quietly resumed her place as the divine mother goddess in the cosmos.

These sons would come to represent the sacred number four. Four is an important number in many Indigenous American mythologies. The quadruplets, who were also referred to as two sets of twins, would come to symbolize the four cardinal directions.

The four brothers heard that Yaya's gourd was full of fish, and they wanted to see this for themselves. They waited until Yaya was out on his lands before sneaking into the house. Once inside, they snatched the gourd from its hanging place on the rafters. Peering inside, they saw the fish, and they began to eat them. Suddenly, they got word that Yaya was returning to his home. Quickly, they tried to hang the gourd back so they could make their escape before getting caught.

The brother, Deminán, was the one tasked with the job of putting the gourd back, but in his haste, the gourd wasn't hung properly, and it fell, crashing to the ground. Out poured the salty tears of Yaya, who had been heartbroken over his son's betrayal and death. In this version of the story, the tears were so numerous that they flowed out across the land, taking the multitudes of colorful fish and other marine life with them.

Deminán.[ii]

The tears pooled and became what we now know as the salty Caribbean Sea, and it was filled with many unique types of fish in all shapes and sizes. The fish became a source of life-sustaining food for the Taíno and all of the people living in the Antilles region. Deminán and his brothers were swept up into the sea. They were separated for a great deal of time before they were able to find each other again.[5]

---

[5] "The Taíno Myth of the Cursed Creator - Bill Keegan." *TED*, TED-Ed, https://ed.ted.com/lessons/the-taino-myth-of-the-cursed-creator-bill-keegan Accessed 15 Mar. 2024.

The Turtle Woman

The quadruplets were cursed to wander the spiritual world upon finding each other once again, trying to find where they came from. Since their mother, Itiba Cahubaba, had died in childbirth, no one had ever explained to them their heritage. They had no idea about their family or had a purpose in life. They did not know that within their souls, they held the magic of the four directions.

The brothers, including Deminán, were known to be troublemakers, playing tricks on their elders and annoying everyone in the community. Stealing Yaya's gourd of tears and his son's bones was only one of their many crimes.

One fateful day, the four brothers went to the door of an old man named Bayamanaco to ask for food. They saw he was carrying casabe, or cassava bread. The brothers said to him, "Ahiacabo guarocoel," which means "Let us meet our grandfather." They ran through the hut, ransacking it and taking food. The old man had been sitting in his hut snorting the powder cohoba (a powerful hallucinogen used ritualistically by the Taíno behiques), which sent him on a journey to mystic realms and made mucus run out of his nose.

A cohoba inhaler.[iii]

The man awoke from his stupor and looked at the boys destroying his home. He quietly raised one palm to the air and then covered one of his nostrils. Turning to Deminán, he took aim and fired the uncovered nostril's mucus and spittle straight onto Deminán's back. The ball of mucus stuck to Deminán. He was absolutely enraged at the old man, and Deminán began screaming and cursing at Bayamanaco.

Meanwhile, the three other brothers noticed something very alarming happening to Deminán's back. The spot where the mucus had landed was turning red. Deminán began to feel it burning.

The boys ran from the hut. They sat and watched Deminán's back as it began to grow redder and more painful. Soon, Deminán was crying in pain, and the spot turned into a quickly growing welt. To their disbelief, the welt grew into a hump. Deminán was writhing in pain and fear by this point while his brothers tried to lance the growing lump, but it didn't help. The lump began to squirm around under his skin. Something was moving inside of Deminán!

The brothers didn't know what to do. Suddenly, the welt erupted, and a giant sea turtle crawled out from the gash on Deminán's humped back. The boys stared with their mouths open as the turtle transformed before their eyes into a beautiful woman. This woman had one unique quality that set her apart from Deminán. She was brimming with compassion, which is exactly what the four brothers were lacking.

The old man had known exactly what the boys needed, and he used the sea turtle to teach them this lesson. As the boys learned compassion from The Turtle Woman, the magic from Bayamanaco worked within them and formed them into one complete human. Before, there had been four dissociated personalities that caused havoc. Now that they had gained compassion, they had all the qualities of a good person.

The Turtle Woman explained to Deminán that their child would possess the full embodiment of the cosmos: the four directions, consisting of the freedom from the prejudice of the south, the inward vision and intuition of the west, the illumination of the east, and the wisdom and experience of the north. Each brother possessed one of these qualities, but now, as one combined being, he would be the foundation for humankind. All of the future people of the Caribbean islands would be his descendants.[6]

---

[6] Taíno Chronicles 8 – Caney Circle -
https://caneycircle.wordpress.com/legends/tainochronicles8/

As the turtle entered the ocean that the brothers had accidentally created by spilling Yaya's gourd of tears, she grew. Her back became the land on which the earth was populated. This is similar to the stories of Turtle Island, which are told by the Indigenous peoples of North and Central America.

With the female turtle, Deminán had created a bridge between the spirit and the human world. He was the first in a long line of mythic Taíno heroes who would continue to connect the human and spirit world together.[7]

Taíno Worldview and Connections

There are alternate versions of this creation myth that you will find later on in this book, including stories of how the oceans came to be and how women were created after men. The myth of Yaya, Yayael, the gourd, and the cursed quadruplets remains the most enduring creation story in the Taíno culture, though.

In the Taíno version of the earliest days on earth, there was a great flood that came from the tears of Yaya. After the great flood, humans populated the planet, living on the land made by the back of the female turtle. This is very similar to the Christian story of the great flood. The Maya, Incas, Aztecs, Chickasaw, Cheyenne, Greeks, Mesopotamians, Chinese, and many other cultures across the planet all have a similar story of a massive flood.

Creation myths of Indigenous Americans also include reverence for the cardinal directions, as we see represented by the four brothers in the Taíno myth. Cultures that speak of the four directions actually span across the globe and include Anemoi of Greek mythology, Bacab of Maya mythology, Dikpālas of Buddhist and Hindu mythology, and the Four Holy Beasts of Vietnamese mythology.

The Taíno people believed that nature was meant to complement their lives and that it should add beauty and interest to their surroundings. This is a sharp contrast to the stereotypical Western worldview, where nature is believed to be something that can be owned and serves a purpose for us rather than existing alongside us in harmony.

---

[7] The Decline of The Taínos 1432 - 1511 - Duke University Thesis - https://teamsocialstudies.uconn.edu/wp-content/uploads/sites/47/2021/04/The-Decline-of-the-Taínos-1492-1542_-A-Re-Vision-1.pdf

The Taíno always tried to respect their surroundings. Each of their stories and beliefs includes a deep appreciation for nature.[8]

While the Taíno are a unique group of people, their creation myths have many parallels to other cultures across the world, especially with the creation stories of other Indigenous cultures in the Americas. As you'll find throughout this book, there are instances of the Taíno traditions inspiring the spirituality of other cultures that they met, interacted, and traded with.

---

[8] Taíno Creation Myth: Ancient Wisdom and Its Relevance in Modern Life | by Finally Detached. Medium. https://medium.com/@finallydetached/taino-creation-myth-ancient-wisdom-and-its-relevance-in-modern-life-e0c0f7f5f8bc.

Chapter 2: Gods and Goddesses: Taíno Entities

Taíno Pantheon

The Taíno have different levels of spirits and gods in their religion. The ones most similar to our traditional definition of gods and goddesses are known as the Zemi, or the great spirit gods. These Zemi are worshiped across the islands with their own dedicated temples. Each of these gods and goddesses has their own domain of creation.

Yúcahu Maórocoti

Yúcahu (also written as Yucáhuguama Bagua Maórocoti, Yukajú, Yocajú, Yokahu, or Yukiyú) is the primary god of the Taíno. He is the son of Atabey, the mother goddess. Yúcahu is the one who formed Earth at the beginning of the creation story. His twin, Guacar, left and went to the earth below and didn't stay to help him in his creation. Yúcahu also opened a rift in the space between the heavens and the earth below, where the cemís (a god-like spirit housed in sculpture form) lived. He called forth cemís to send to the earth below, a few at a time, to carry out tasks on Earth.

Yúcahu is known for creating cassava or yucca, a life-sustaining food. He's also revered for creating the hutia, a now-extinct large rodent resembling a rat or squirrel, and sweet potatoes. He was known for his power to grow successful crops. He lives on Yu-Ke, a mountain in Borikén. Yu-ke (also spelled Yuké) translates to "white lands," and

Borikén is what the Taíno called the present-day island of Puerto Rico, a name that is still used occasionally by locals.[9]

In later myths, Yúcahu bleeds his body in order to create many gods, leading him to sometimes be referred to as the god of male fertility or representative of male menstruation.[10]

Yúcahu takes on the mortal form of a tall, muscular man, although some say he looks like an elder statesman wearing fine silks. In artistic depictions of him, he is frequently carrying a yucca root and an ax. His name translates to "soul of the yucca plant."

The yucca root once was the most important crop for the people of the Caribbean islands. Every culture around the world has a plant that is high in starch and sustains life for their culture. Many cultures eat wheat or bread. In Asia, rice is the staple high-carbohydrate food, while many Indigenous Americans utilize corn. Some cultures have potatoes. The people of the Caribbean kept themselves alive with the power of yucca.

It is said that Yúcahu came to rest on top of El Yunque on Borikén, where he still lives. From there, he keeps the realm of the cemís connected to the earthly realm. Legend has it that he stays on the mountaintop to fight off storms from Guabancex and Juracán, slicing into their hurricanes and protecting the people who live down below.[11]

Atabey

Atabey, which can also be spelled as Atabei or Atabeira, is the creator of the universe. No one knows where she came from. Some say that she birthed herself into being.

Atabey is a loving maternal goddess. She has twin sons, Yúcahu and Guacar. She gave her sons the power to create so that they could continue filling the universe with life. Atabey lives in the cosmos, far away in the stars, in peace.

She takes many forms, famously coming to Earth for a time as a woman named Itiba Cahubaba, who sacrificed herself in a bloody birth when her quadruplet sons were born. After she died in childbirth, she returned to the stars as Atabey. Guabancex, the god of storms and violence, who you will read about next, is a form of Atabey.

---

[9] "Discover History" - https://www.fs.usda.gov/r08/elyunque/recreation/discover-history

[10] "Tradition of the Male Harsh Menstruation Spirit." https://indigenouscaribbean.ning.com/m/blogpost?id=2030313%3ABlogPost%3A67964

[11] "El Yunque: Its History." *El Yunque Inns*, www.elyunqueinns.com/el-yunque-its-history.

On Earth, Atabey holds power over the rains, the oceans, and the fish. If she appears, she will look like an older woman carrying a gourd filled with water, just like the one that Yaya kept his tears of sorrow in, which later became the waters of the ocean.

Guabancex

Atabey has several manifestations, including the spirit of love called Caguana and Guabancex or Guabancesh, who is the violent counterpart to Atabey's loving mother figure. Guabancex brings about storms, volcanoes, and earthquakes. She is accompanied by two male spirits: Guataubá, who controls thunder and lightning, and Coatrisque, who is the ruler of torrential rains and causes great floods and heavy precipitation.

Guabancex can be easily confused with Juracán, as they fulfill similar roles. While they are actually two separate deities, some debate remains in certain circles that they may be one.

Guabancex is the destructive female counterpart to Atabey's loving mother energy. They are both supreme goddesses and matriarchal representations of Mother Nature in a mirror image of each other. The great mother goddess can create life and also wipe it away with wild storms.

Juracán represents whirling storms (his name is a form of the word "hurricane"), and he serves under Guabancex. This is explained by the fact that Juracán was originally one of Atabey's twin sons, while Guabancex is a form of Atabey herself. The powers of Guabancex branch far, as she controls all destructive natural elements, including earthquakes, volcanoes, and even climate shifts.

Guabancex continually reminds humanity how vulnerable we are to natural disasters.[12] She also reminds us that no one can ever conquer nature, no matter how strong they may be.

Guabancex is frequently represented as an erupting volcano; however, instead of being in the shape of a mountain, the volcano is presented in the shape of a female breast. Her sacred animal is the serpent, which snakes out from the breast-shaped volcano in the form of lava, lying at the bottom with its mouth gaping wide open, baring its sharp teeth. She sometimes appears as a tall, muscular woman. She always carries a

---

[12] The Identity of GuaBanCex, Spirit of Natural Disasters. Indigenous Caribbean Network - https://indigenouscaribbean.ning.com/profiles/blogs/the-identity-of-guabancex-spirit-of-natural-disasters

sharpened spear, and her face is painted as if she's ready for war. She's also known as the lover of Juracán; together, they cause chaos, even ruining friendships and marriages out of boredom. You can read more about Guabancex and how she appears in the myths of the Taíno culture in Chapter 7.

Karaya

Karaya is the moon spirit. The moon spirit represents the twenty-eight-day menstrual cycle, a vital part of the mother goddess's fertility. Karaya the moon spirit represents the link between human women and the cosmic woman, Atabey. The link between human women and Atabey is celebrated with the full moon ceremony. Some say that Yúcahu represents male fertility. Karaya is not to be confused with Maroya, the goddess of the moon.[13]

Juracán

Formally known as Guacar, Juracán is the twin brother of Yúcahu. The twin brothers were created by Atabey, the supreme mother goddess.

Juracán was known for his vindictiveness and shared the ability to whip up storms with Guabancex. The legend of Coquí and the goddess lets us know just how far Juracán would go to get his way. Coquí was the handsome son of a brilliant cacique. He was so handsome that he caught the attention of a goddess, who quickly fell in love with him.

The goddess rewarded Coquí with successful hunting and fishing trips frequently, and Coquí would thank her by breaking into song, his voice carrying clearly over the mountains. She loved him too much to stay away, though she knew that the other gods would not take kindly to her falling in love with a human.

One night, she took the form of a human woman and appeared before Coquí, who recognized her as the goddess of his dreams. Their love was undeniable, but when Juracán took notice, trouble came to paradise. Juracán pulled together a wicked storm, filling the sky with dark storm clouds.

There was nothing the goddess could do to save Coquí. Juracán was too strong, and he pulled Coquí away, never to be found again. Devastated, the goddess did the only thing she could think to do with her

---

[13] "Indigenous Caribbean Network." *TRADITION OF THE MALE HARSH MENSTRUATION SPIRIT,* indigenouscaribbean.ning.com/m/blogpost?id=2030313%3ABlogPost%3A67964

grief. She poured what she could remember of Coquí's beautiful voice into a tiny creature. To this day, frogs hop around the Caribbean, calling out the name of the man the goddess would never stop loving. "Coquí! Coquí!"[14]

Guataubá

Guataubá is known as the god of clouds and the harbinger of the strong winds that come with fierce storms. He works for Guabancex, assisting in bringing deadly gusts across the earth. Guataubá always ruins Atabey's work. As soon as Atabey makes the ocean smooth like glass, creating a peaceful and sunny afternoon, Guataubá blows huge bursts of winds to stir up the water, making the ocean rough and dangerous.

When Guataubá appears in human form, he looks like a boy in puberty just before reaching manhood. He carries a frond from the palm tree. Guataubá uses this frond to create wind and waves, ripping the seas into a frenzy.

Coatrisque

Coatrisque is a goddess and the sibling of Guataubá. She rules the waters. The pair of siblings work in tandem to help Guabancex create storms. Coatrisque is mischievous and causes purposeful harm to humans. She waits for Guataubá to create the waves with his wind, and then she uses an oar to direct the waves toward humans who are in the water going about their lives. She causes their canoes to capsize. At times, she manages to flood entire islands, causing death and complete destruction to people's homes.

Representations of water birds, such as herons or cormorants, are frequently associated with Coatrisque. They are said to do her bidding, carrying storm waters wherever Coatrisque tells them to.

While Coatrisque is sometimes referred to as a male entity, she is more often than not referred to as a woman. Coatrisque always appears in human form as a woman with an oar. She uses the oar to direct the waves, and when she's not doing that, she will use her oar to point her brother Guataubá toward the seas that Atabey has recently calmed so that the duo can get to work wreaking their havoc.

---

[14] "Coqui – Encantada: Isle of Myths." *ENCANTADA Isle of Myths*, mitosencantado.com/coqui/

Maquetaurie Guayaba

Maquetaurie Guayaba is known as the Lord of the Dead. He is the cacique of Coaybay, which is the Taíno underworld. He is associated with the west, which is the land of the setting sun, bringing darkness to the land and releasing the spirits into the night. The Taíno portrayed Maquetaurie Guayaba as a tired-looking middle-aged man. They picture him leaning over stonework and writings, which is how he sorts all of the lives of the dead. The later Taíno credited him with inventing writing and said he kept it a secret for many years.

The second half of his name, "Guayaba," is also the Taíno word for the fruit guava, which is perhaps a reference to the myths of the *opías* (or *hupía*, spirits of the dead), who frequently come out at night to feast on the fruit.

The owl and bat are frequently used as symbols of Maquetaurie Guayaba and are seen as spirits of the dead by the Taíno. More information on this is outlined in Chapter 7.

Opiyelguabirán

Opiyelguabirán is a wild-looking god with the body of a dog and the head of a man. He drags the dead into the realm of Coaybay. He has dense hair full of mats, and his nails are so long that the Taíno say they're the length of actual spears.

Opiyelguabirán doesn't speak the same language as the Taíno. His words are unintelligible. Although he seems to babble, Maquetaurie, the Lord of the Dead, can still understand him. When Taíno dancers were getting ready to dance, the dancers would often pray to him for wild energy and stamina.

It is said that the Taíno tried to catch him with ropes, but he always managed to get away. When the Spanish and Christians arrived, legend has it that Opiyelguabirán ran and ran, escaping to a private lagoon. As much as the surviving Taíno tried to look for him, he was nowhere to be found. He remains lost to this day.[15]

---

[15] Dubois, Laurent. *Haiti Reader: History, Culture, Politics*. Duke University Press, 2020. - https://cowlatinamerica.voices.wooster.edu/wp-content/uploads/sites/263/2021/03/j.ctv1220qc0.5.pdf

Racuno, Sobaco, Achinao, and Coromo

Yúcahu found four gemstones lying on the ground. He picked them up and filled them with life. He tossed them into the air, and they immediately flew into the heavens, away from Earth. They became the four stars in the sky that went on to birth all of the other stars.

They also created the birds, which were meant to be their partners in the sky. Hummingbirds are closely associated with these four brothers. The birds fly between the human realm and the realms belonging to the cemís. Shooting stars that can be seen in the sky on a dark night are supposedly the messages being transported by the birds between the realms.

Racuno, Sobaco, Achinao, and Coromo appear as typical Greater Antillean island male figures. They each look identical to each other, yet they are each dressed in different colors to tell them apart. Racuno loves orange. Sobaco prefers yellow. Coromo is represented by a deep blue hue, and Achinao wears the color red.

The brothers are known for their wit and their boisterous personalities, as well as their speed and agility. They are often called the Star Quartet. Many believe that the four brothers find Taíno people wherever they have been scattered on Earth, connecting them back to their ancestral roots.[16]

Maroya

Maroya is the goddess of the moon, though in some writings, Maroya is referred to as a god rather than a goddess. In the male form, Maroya takes the name Márohu. She chases her brother, Boinayel, the god of the sun, across the sky, appearing as a small silver sliver in comparison to his bright yellow brilliance. When Maroya appears in the sky, she brings the cool darkness of night to the earth. Her dim light is not for the sleeping Taíno people; it's actually for the spirits of the dead that walk the earth in the dark.

The spirits of the dead who live in the beautiful realm called Coaybay are able to roam the earth under the dim glow of the moon. But what about those who died that aren't worthy of entering Coaybay? Those spirits are known as *opias*, and they must stay in the places of darkness where Maroya and her moonlight can't reach. They lurk under the

---

[16] Zemi (Taíno) Pantheon For Scion 1e | PDF | Christopher Columbus
https://www.scribd.com/document/644730208/Zemi-Taíno -Pantheon-For-Scion-1e

darkness of dense trees, in the rocky areas behind waterfalls, or in caves. They often take the form of owls and bats.

The *opías* can change into human form as well. They attempt to sneak into villages, tricking humans by sweet-talking the youth in an attempt to find lovers. Once they capture a human, they will kill them in an attempt to bring them over to their miserable existence. Maroya will hunt these spirits down and attempt to stop them before they can kill anyone. She will strike them with her arrows before locking them away into oblivion.

If Maroya ever manages to catch up to her brother, then an eclipse will appear in the sky as the two cross paths. Maroya appears as a tall woman. She is very athletic and beautiful, with black hair cascading down her back.

Boinayel

Boinayel was Yúcahu's first son, and he was also the sun god. Boinayel is the brother of Maroya. He spent a lot of time with her racing back and forth across the open sky above the earth for eons before humans appeared on the planet.

Long ago, when the first Taíno lived in their ancestral cave called Cacibajagua, there was a guardian at the cave entrance who was late returning to his duties. When Boinayel saw the cave unguarded, he decided to trick the guardian by luring him out of the dark cave to bask in his beautiful light. Once he had him in the open, he turned him into all of the animals, plant life, and trees that cover the islands. There were still humans remaining in the cave. They went on to become the Taíno people. In another version of this myth, Boinayel turns the guardian into stone so that he may never close his eyes on the cave again.

Once the humans entered the world, Boinayel was very kind to them. He led them to good land, and he showed them the wonders of agriculture so that they could take care of themselves and live well.

Boinayel, in his human form, appears as a younger man with dark skin. He carries a shiny sphere, which represents the sun as a cemí. He is kind, benevolent, and a trickster.

Guacar

Guacar saw what his mother and brother had created and became mad with jealousy. He transformed himself into the evil spirit Juracán (or Hurricane), and with the help of his wife, Guabancex (goddess of storms), and his two sons (representing thunder and lightning), they stirred up catastrophic stormy winds to destroy his family's creations.[17] His raging tempests killed animals and destroyed Locuo's crops, but he could not unmake the earth. Locuo (the first human man) prayed to the gods to spare him so his family would be saved.

Though Guacar was responsible for the raging storms that threatened Locuo's way of life, some say that the god actually was teaching Locuo valuable lessons about how to survive. Because of the storms and tribulations that Locuo was put through, humans were able to gain the knowledge necessary to protect themselves and their crops.

Guacar is known as the patron god of warriors. He is associated with his two weapons, the wooden makana, which is a sword, and a manaya, which is a stone-bladed hatchet. The Taínos also consider a dagger to be representative of Guacar.

He is considered to be the god of the north because north is related to wisdom on the Taíno sacred medicine wheel. Since Guacar is a warrior and is willing to sacrifice himself, he is considered to have been wise since utilizing one's wisdom never comes without making a sacrifice.

---

[17] Gods and Goddesses: Tales of The Taino: https://thevalelondon.co.uk/blogs/the-vale-articles/gods-and-goddesses-tales-of-the-taino#:~:text=Guacar%2C%20on%20the%20other%20hand,Caribbean%20hurricane%20myth%20was%20born

Chapter 3: Animal Spirits and Their Role in Taíno Myth

The Taíno traditional beliefs lend a high level of respect to nature for the wisdom it contains, including the animal kingdom. The Taíno believe that there are three levels to the spirit realm, and animals are present at each level.[18]

Turey is the upper realm. This is the sky world above the land where Atabey resides. Ku is the middle realm. This is the surface of the earth. The Taíno believe the earth is resting on the back of a turtle, much as the Maya believed it rested on the back of a kaiman, or the Earth Crocodile. Below the earth exists the realm of Coaybay, the underworld. It is filled with spirits and ghosts of the dead.

Every type of animal on the islands has a role to play in Taíno spirituality. The sacred medicine wheel is the first thing to learn about when examining the role of animals in the Taíno religion and belief system.

The medicine wheel is called Guaiko and contains the four cardinal directions as part of twenty-eight total units that are typically represented visually by stones. The four cardinal directions are said to be the original four stones cast into the sky at the beginning of time that became the four stars to represent north, south, east, and west. Each cardinal

---

[18] Animals – Caney Circle https://caneycircle.wordpress.com/animals/

direction has its own animal, a type of sacred bird. The cardinal directions also each possess its own color and food.[19]

North is overseen by the beautiful hummingbird named babae. The hummingbird's spiritual gift is the wisdom that comes from experience. It harvests cassava bread, which is made from yucca. The bread is white, so the color of the north is also white. The name of the northern star is Rakuno.

South is represented by the turkey, called *guanaho* by the Taíno. The turkey harvests green squash, associated with Taíno in the southern region. The spiritual gifts from the south are innocence and open-mindedness. The name of the southern star is Achiano.

East is represented by the hawk, called *guaraguao*. The hawk harvests yellow maize, or corn, and brings the spiritual gift of illumination, enlightenment, farsightedness, and the gift of travel. The enlightenment a hawk has can be achieved by finding a perfect balance in your life. The name of the eastern star is Sobaiko.

West is represented by the owl, interchangeably called *múcaro*, who harvests black beans. The owl gives the spiritual gift of introspection, which allows humans to look deeper into their own soul and further inside the spirit world, just as the owl's large eyes allow it to see clearly in the darkness of night. The owl is a symbol of death, as is the bat. The name of the western star is Koromo.

These spiritual gifts of the cardinal directions are the four main virtues that the Taíno strived to follow in their daily lives: wisdom, open-mindedness, enlightenment, and introspection. We can clearly see how animals played an integral role in Taíno spirituality since they are tied into every area of the Taíno belief system.

The Taíno believed strongly in learning information about nature by observing animals. For example, the Taíno mimicked the behavior of birds when sailing out on the open seas. The *Tijereta Sabanera*, which is Spanish for "fork-tailed flycatcher," is a bird that floats on thermals above the ocean. The bird finds rising currents of warm air and happily floats and swoops in them.

If the Taíno saw a large amount of the Tijereta Sabanera enjoying currents of warm air, they knew a tropical storm was developing or a hurricane was coming because rising warm air is what fuels tropical

---

[19] Medicine Wheel – Caney Circle https://caneycircle.wordpress.com/wheel/

storms. The Taíno also recognized that the Tijereta Sabanera stayed close to the shoreline. When they were out sailing and started seeing Tijereta Sabanera, they knew the land would be just over the horizon.

Migratory birds also helped the Taíno keep track of their calendar. They recognized the patterns in the comings and goings of the birds and used that to know when seasons were changing or to judge how much time had passed.

There are many stories and connotations attached to each common animal found on the Antillean Islands. Here are a few more details about them.

The Hawk

Perhaps one of the most vital animals in Taíno spirituality is the hawk. The hawk is the personification of the Great Spirit, Yaya, and the cardinal direction of the east. The hawk is said to carry prayers to the Great Spirit.

In folklore and Taíno myths, the hawk appears in the story of how the owl came to be a nocturnal animal. During the times of good harvests and no drought, the animals would celebrate as much as possible. With the stormy season approaching, the birds decided to throw one last big party with more animals than had ever been invited before.

All the fastest birds were called upon to fly around and distribute the party invitations to all the different animals. The red-tailed hawk took this task particularly seriously, flying as fast as he could to make sure that each and every animal was invited to the party. Perhaps he had been left out from time to time himself, so he wanted to ensure no one else ever felt that way.

Everyone that the red-tailed hawk invited to the party reacted with excitement—except for the owl. In fact, it seemed like the owl hardly cared about the red-tailed hawk's invitation. Instead, he moped around in his nest, ducking his beak away from the light. As the red-tailed hawk hopped closer for a better look, he saw that the owl was completely naked.

Worried that the owl was going to get cold, the red-tailed hawk leaned in. "Excuse me, Owl, but are you all right? You're...naked!"

Ashamed, the owl nodded. "I don't have any clothes. Not a single bit of fur or feather to wear. That's why I can't go to the party. Imagine me showing up like this. No one would come near me, and they'd all talk behind my back."

Appalled, the red-tailed hawk knew he had to do something. He couldn't stand by while the owl suffered, knowing that he had plenty of feathers himself.

"Wait right here. I'm going to figure something out!" the red-tailed hawk promised. Then, he flew as fast as he could back to where the birds congregated, explaining the difficult situation their friend was in. Everyone listened, shocked to hear that the owl was in such a poor state.

"I hate the idea of Owl missing the party just because he doesn't have anything to wear! I have an idea for something that just might help. Because we all want to help, don't we?" the red-tailed hawk asked the group.

Everyone squawked and tweeted their approval. "Good! I was thinking that we all pluck out one or two of our own feathers and gather them all together. Then, Owl will be able to make something for himself to wear."

"As long as he promises to give the feathers back, I can't see the harm," the parrot said, wanting to be generous and help the owl while still protecting his own interests.

After deciding that it was a good plan, all the birds did as they were told, happily handing over their beautiful plumage so that the owl would be able to join them at the party. When the red-tailed hawk delivered the stunning package to the owl, he was deeply moved and thanked the hawk and his friends for their generous gift.

"You're all too kind. I'll, of course, return all the feathers the very next day," Owl swore.

Owl worked through the nights to finish creating an outfit for himself, fanning the feathers around his big eyes and making a cape. When it came time for the party, he strutted around proudly, showing off his new and impressive plumage, which was more varied and thicker than anyone else's.

The next day, as everyone recovered from the long, celebratory evening, the owl replayed his glory. It felt so good to have such wonderful clothes and be graced with so many compliments. Though he knew it was time to return the thoughtful gift the red-tailed hawk had organized for him, the owl couldn't bring himself to do it.

At first, the rest of the birds gave the owl the benefit of the doubt, trusting that the feathers would be returned by the week's end. The owl, however, had a very different idea of what was going to happen. Determined to keep his new clothes, the owl started avoiding everyone else. He kept to himself and hunted at night instead of the day, hiding in the trees and keeping out of sight, all to avoid returning the feathers that had been generously loaned to him.

Though the other birds looked for the owl, no one ever found him. Occasionally, the owl could be heard calling out under the protection of night, reminding everyone else of what he had taken from them.

The Hutia

What exactly is a hutia? This animal is a large rodent similar to the groundhog or marmot. There are several species labeled as hutia, including a smaller type that lives in the trees and a larger type that lives in burrows underground like the North American groundhog. The animal has a long tail, similar to a rat.

There are many varieties of hutia, though almost half of them have gone extinct since the days of the Taíno. The largest of the hutia species, the giant hutia, is included on the list of extinct animals. While the animal bore similarities to a rat, it is said that the giant hutia of the time looked more like the modern capybara.

Because of the burrowing habits of the largest hutia species, the Taíno believed the hutia helped the shaman along his journey into the lower realm, Coaybay. The hutia was able to guide the shaman through the maze of tunnels until he reached the open space of the lower world, where he was then able to move about freely in order to learn and grow spiritually.

As such, there is some evidence that the Taíno domesticated the hutia. The findings of archaeologists and scientists researching Taíno settlements found the remains of hutia and fencing that might have been used as a corral. The contents discovered in the stomachs of the animals suggested that the hutia had been eating similar foods to that of the Taíno people. By extension of that, it can either be assumed that the Taíno were purposefully feeding the animals or that the hutias were scavenging through waste. In Hispaniola, there are stories of hutia being kept in corrals.[20]

---

[20] "Human and Hutia (Isolobodon Portoricensis) Interactions in Pre-Columbian Hispaniola: The

Hutias were also a source of food for the Taíno people, which might have been another reason to domesticate or farm the animals. If it were not for the fact that the hutia is now an endangered species, some traditionalist Taíno people would still be hunting it.

Scientists consider the existence of the hutia as evidence that the islands were once part of a larger continent, possibly South America, because these land rodents normally only exist on the mainland rather than on isolated islands. Evidence shows the hutias were present on the islands for thousands of years, making it unlikely they were introduced by humans traveling or trading, unlike other animals, such as the jaguar or turkey.[21]

The Hummingbird

Hummingbirds are delicate, elusive creatures. For the Taíno, they are the embodiment of wisdom and experience. The Taíno word for hummingbird is *colibri*. The hummingbird represents north on the medicine wheel, which is known as the realm of experience.

The Taíno considered the hummingbird's plumage to represent the rainbow. For the Taíno, the rainbow was a bridge between the land, sky, and underworld in the cosmos. Only the most highly respected animals could move between these realms.[22]

On the islands, the Taíno noticed the tiniest hummingbirds could be the size of an insect. These types of hummingbirds are known as bee hummingbirds or *guani*. The word *guani* makes up the word *guanín,* a gold and copper alloy that was fashioned into circular pendants that the cacique wore.

There were many species of hummingbirds on the islands, most of which had names beginning with the prefix "zum" or "zun," which sound like the noise a hummingbird makes as it zooms past.[23]

Hummingbirds have a unique way of flying that allows them to hover in one spot, inserting their long beaks to extract the sweet nectar from

---

Isotopic and Morphological Evidence - ScienceDirect" -
https://www.sciencedirect.com/science/article/pii/S2352409X21001255

[21] Dominican Republic: Knowing a Colorful Country from Deep Inside.
https://mocacity.blogspot.com/2011/04/dominican-republic-knowing-colorful.html

[22] Times of the Islands – Talking Taíno: Birds of a Feather.
https://www.timespub.tc/2006/01/talking-Taíno-birds-of-a-feather/

[23] Times of the Islands – Talking Taíno: Birds of a Feather.
https://www.timespub.tc/2006/01/talking-Taíno-birds-of-a-feather/

the flower. They are the only birds that can fly forward, backward, sideways, and up and down. The Taíno recognized just how special of a species they were, hence their ability to travel between the realms.

In Taíno folklore, the hummingbird's flight style has a heartbreaking origin. As the story goes, Alida, a beautiful young woman, went down to the watering hole by herself one day. There, she caught the eye of a handsome young man who happened to be from a neighboring tribe. They got to talking straight away, each caught in the beauty of each other's eyes.

There, by the pool surrounded by a small clearing filled with red flowers, with hummingbirds flitting from blossom to blossom, Alida and Taroo fell in love. When Alida eventually told her father of her love, hoping to someday start a life with Taroo, he flew into a rage. Alida was expected to wed someone from her own tribe, and it was a betrayal to think of her marrying someone outside their world, perhaps from a rival Carib tribe.

Immediately, Alida's father started looking for a more appropriate husband for her, and he soon found one. Alida was a beautiful young woman from a respected family, so it was not hard for her father to find someone worthy. Panicked, Alida begged her father to reconsider.

"Please, Baba, you know I'm in love with someone else. Don't break my heart like this," Alida pleaded.

Her father shook his head sharply. "It's already settled, Alida. You will marry the man I have chosen for you in two weeks' time."

There was no persuading him. Alida was either going to have to give up the love of her life or risk losing her family forever. Panicked, Alida went back to the pool where she'd first met Taroo. There, she knelt before a cemí, asking for advice and hoping the gods would have a solution for her.

"Please, I can't marry him! Do what you can to deliver me from this fate, even if it brings me death!" she cried out.

This time, the gods answered her prayers, though not in the way Alida would ever have expected or wanted. They turned her into one of the red flowers that grew on the bank of the pool, abandoned there, unable to speak to or kiss her lover again.

Taroo noticed her absence almost immediately. Each night, he went to see her by their usual meeting place at the pool, waiting as the stars twinkled down on him pityingly. Taroo had no idea that Alida's father forbade their relationship or was forcing her to marry someone else. As far as he knew, Alida had fallen out of love with him, and yet, he still waited each night, hoping to see her.

Eventually, the moon grew tired of the way Taroo was bemoaning Alida's absence.

"Hey, you down there!" the moon called to Taroo.

"Me?" Taroo replied, surprised to see the silver circle in the sky speaking to him.

"It doesn't matter how long you wait. She's never going to come meet you."

"How do you know?"

"Because the gods turned her into that flower there," the moon explained, pointing down at where Alida was standing, her petals fluttering in the evening breeze sadly. Realizing what had happened, Taroo rushed to Alida's side, devastated to find her frozen in flower form.

Desperate to be closer to Alida, Taroo called out to the gods, begging them just as his love had only weeks earlier. Taroo didn't know what he wanted the gods to do exactly, but he knew he couldn't go on without Alida in his life. He needed to find her once more.

Once again, the gods answered the call in their own way, turning Taroo into a hummingbird. That way, he would be able to be close to his love, hovering above her at all times and communicating his love with a hum while she gave him her nectar. It was because of that hum that the Taíno people named the beautiful bird the hummingbird.

In some versions of the story, the moon doesn't tell Taroo exactly which red flower is his beloved. Becoming a hummingbird allowed Taroo to search for Alida more easily, flitting from flower to flower as he searched for the woman who had his heart, though there's no saying how long it might take him to find Alida.

The Puerto Rican folktale has lasted through the years, remaining relevant to pop culture. When the Puerto Rican-born singer Jennifer Lopez released her video album, *This Is Me Now*, in 2024, it included the legend of Alida and Taroo in the prologue of the film.[24]

---

[24] "J-Lo's 'This Is Me...Now: A Love Story': Is the Hummingbird Legend Real? A Historian Weighs In." TODAY.Com

The Owl

The Taíno word for owl is *múcaro*, which means eagle of the night. Thanks to the folktale about the naked owl who stole everyone's feathers, the owl is known as a thief, but that is just the beginning of the bird's dark reputation.

The múcaro represents the direction west in the medicine wheel. The west is the place where the sun disappears, leaving the people shrouded in the darkness of the night. The Taíno attributed the owl to Maquetaurie Guayaba, the god of death and the divine world.

The Taíno believed that the souls of the dead (*opias*) could walk the earth at night, though they needed to take a new form in order to do so. Sometimes, they would take the form of a human, even going as far as to seduce the living, though one hug from a human would make them disappear, sending them back to the land of the dead on the other side of the island.

The spirits of the dead also frequently transformed into owls or bats. The dark caves that bats and owls frequently live in were comforting for the spirits, and in the form of an owl or person, they could even enjoy a meal again as if they had been given life once more. It is said that the *opias* were especially attracted to guavas and other sweet fruits, just like bats.

Owls can be found on pottery and are easily recognized by their large, circular eyes. Considering that owls in the Caribbean often live in caves, it follows that the Taíno held owls in high spiritual regard considering the significance of caves in their culture. As mentioned, Taíno saw the owl as a zoomorphic, or animal-like version, of a deceased spirit or ghost.[25]

Amongst the owl-inspired pottery that has been discovered over the years, an owl-shaped ceremonial pestle has been found, leading experts to believe that it might have been used to crush cohoba powder for use by behiques in rituals, as the owl was considered a powerful spirit with connections to the dead.

From time to time, the Taíno shamans would use owls in an attempt to cure the very ill or bring the recently dead back to life. Not only was the call of the owl considered a death prophecy, but the Taíno also believed they could use owls to tempt the *opias* (spirits) to take back

---

[25] Times of the Islands – Talking Taíno: Birds of a Feather
https://www.timespub.tc/2006/01/talking-Taíno-birds-of-a-feather/

their human form and revive the patient.[26]

It has been noted that the owl is sometimes overshadowed by or confused with the bat in Taíno mythology. They play similar roles as guides to the underworld and animals who represent imminent death. Both often linger in caves and dark places and only come out at night. One potential theory to explain this relates to the changing flora and fauna of the area. Where bats were more common than owls, they might have taken on a greater significance over the other.[27]

The Taíno are not the only Indigenous people to consider the owl to be a harbinger of death. Other nations, such as the Kwakwaka'wakw in British Columbia, Canada, believe that those near to death may be able to hear the owl calling their name as they fly overhead, welcoming them to the darkness. The Pueblo tribes of the American Southwest hold similar beliefs.

The connection between owls and death ventures even farther afield, stretching all the way to Europe. The ancient Greeks often depicted their goddess of war, Athena, with an owl in her possession, strengthening the bond between owls and destruction. Other European traditions often describe owls as frequent companions of witches.

Similar to the Taíno belief that an owl could guide a soul back into a body, the ancient Egyptians thought that the owl could shepherd a soul to the afterlife, given its ability to fly into the dark unknown without the need for light.

In Taíno mythology, the nighttime is when danger is most present. Everyone is sleeping except for the *opias*, the spirits of the forest. The birds of the night hold a special place in Taíno culture. In addition to owls, other birds of the night include the yellow-crowned night heron, known as the *yaboa*, which emits a shocking squawking noise when startled in the dark, and the nighthawk, which is called the *querequete*.

---

[26] "Rare Taíno Stone Ceremonial Axe Owl Form" Artemis Gallery - https://www.bidsquare.com/online-auctions/artemis-gallery/rare-Ta%C3%ADno%20-stone-ceremonial-axe-owl-form-2533380

[27] Antillean Islander Space: On the Religious Beliefs and Representations of the Taíno People. - https://www.researchgate.net/publication/295088890_Antillean_Islander_Space_On_the_Religious_Beliefs_and_Representations_of_the_Taino_People

The Parrot

Today, the Puerto Rican parrot, also known as the *iguaca*, is a critically endangered species.[28] There are 250 remaining Puerto Rican Amazon parrots (the only parrot that still exists and is native to Puerto Rico) on the island today. Conservation efforts began in 1968 and are still currently underway to breed more of these beautiful green birds.[29]

Back in the heyday of the Taíno, parrots flourished in the area, though there were always disasters that threatened their population. Hurricanes and other storms have long been common in the area. When the storms got particularly bad, the Taínos would rush into the Luquillo Mountains for safety, following the parrots. From there, they could pray to the god Yúcahu for clearer weather. Even now, this is still where parrots in the area flee to when the winds pick up.[30]

The parrot played not only an important role in Taíno mythology but also in trade for the entirety of the West Indies. Parrot feathers could be used to make colorful crowns and were also used in a pendant. The pendant had vertical holes carved into stone that the feathers could be pushed into to create a fan-like piece of jewelry.

Of course, considering the beauty of the bird and its unique talent for mimicking human speech patterns, the parrot was wanted all over the world. The Spanish explorer Gonzalo Fernández de Oviedo reported that up to twelve different varieties of parrots were shipped back to Spain for King Ferdinand.

There are two Taíno folktales where the parrot appears, and they both happen to be dueling versions of how the rainbow was created. The first version features the handsome Yobuenahuaboshka, who was known for his cleverness and luck. After Yobuenahuaboshka's head was cut off by local dwarves, he still managed to roll his head home, though none of his friends or family were interested in being around a decapitated head.

Agreeing to turn into something else and make himself scarce, Yobuenahuaboshka's only condition was that he be transformed into

---

[28] The Puerto Rican Parrot. https://eynf.oncell.com/en/the-puerto-rican-parrot-145643.html

[29] A New Step Forward in the Future Recovery of the Puerto Rican Parrot | U.S. Fish & Wildlife Service. - https://www.fws.gov/press-release/2022-03/new-step-forward-future-recovery-puerto-rican-parrot

[30] Wildlife, Defenders of. "El Yunque National Forest and the Puerto Rican Parrot: A Story of Peril and Perseverance." - https://medium.com/wild-without-end/el-yunque-national-forest-and-the-puerto-rican-parrot-a-story-of-peril-and-perseverance-d3a37a07fcf2

something that did not yet exist. As such, he took seven balls of colored thread and threw them high into the sky, hooking them up behind the clouds. Then, he braided the threads and climbed up, becoming the moon and the rainbow, two elements that had not existed before.

Some versions of the story include a young woman seated on the shore who looked up just in time to see the colorful rainbow threads. In her moment of distraction, the parrot swooped down and pecked in between the young woman's legs, making her bleed and thus starting the very first cycle of menstruation, which is dictated by the moon.

The conflicting or alternative origin story of the rainbow featuring the parrot can be read below in the section dedicated to the bat.

What role did the parrot play for the Taíno people? The parrot was considered the representation of a classic guardian spirit and thought of as the hallmark symbol of all spirit guides.[31] Parrots were some of the Taíno people's only domesticated animals and were also used as trading goods, but there's evidence that the birds were employed as decoys when hunting.[32]

The Iguana

The word "iguana" derives etymologically from the Taíno word *iwana.* Iguana meat became a delicacy for the Taíno people, eventually becoming so scarce that only the highest-level chiefs were honored with it. In fact, the preciousness of iguanas might be reflected in the word itself. In the Taíno language, the words for gold, parrots, and fire all contain the syllable "gua."

Researchers have been able to determine from fossils dated back to when the Taíno people were first settling in the area that iguanas once stretched to as long as three feet long, though nothing like the giant reptiles of the time exist now.[33]

In Taíno mythology, the iguana is a representation of the Milky Way Galaxy. The Taíno could see the iguana outlined as a constellation among the stars overhead and considered it a representation of the great mother spirit, Atabey. In cave art and pictographs, the image of the

---

[31] Animals – Caney Circle - https://caneycircle.wordpress.com/animals/
[32] Taíno | History & Culture | Britannica. https://www.britannica.com/topic/Taíno.
[33] Keegan, William F., and Lisabeth A. Carlson. Talking Taíno: Essays on Caribbean Natural History from a Native Perspective. - https://www.yumpu.com/en/document/read/65035176/talking-taino-caribbean-natural-history-from-a-native-perspective

iguana often represents the sun, a reference to the way iguanas love to lounge in the bright light.

The mouth of the iguana is a symbol of the sacred cave that the Taíno emerged from, otherwise known as the womb of Atabey. This is the same cave that the sun and the moon come out of each day and night, according to the Taíno creation legend. The cave is named for Iguanaboína, the Great Mother Serpent, a mythical fusion of the iguana and snake.

A Taíno myth about the lizard and iguana explains that the origin of the rock iguanas that sun themselves on the shores and outside the caves on the islands lies with an individual named Macoel. He was assigned to be the nighttime guardian of the sacred cave where the first Taíno people emerged.

Macoel was a lizard-like reptile. He sat as still as a statue outside of the cave, camouflaged by the rocks. He became an unflinching guardian of the area. His name translates to "he of the eyes that do not blink."

You may be wondering how Macoel got his non-blinking eyes. This happened one evening when Macoel was caught not performing his duties as the guard of the cave. Likely on his way back into the cave while the moon was taking over, the sun noticed that Macoel was sleeping. Without a proper guard for the cave, any number of spirits could have been able to escape! The depths of the dark cave were where the souls of the recently departed disappeared to, sometimes represented by the bats and owls that frequented the shadowy corners.

"What do you think you're doing? If you don't watch the entrance, then anyone or anything could escape or, worse, wander in. This is your job, Macoel! You should never be closing your eyes," the sun railed.

Instead, Macoel rolled his eyes. "Hardly anyone comes by here except for you and the moon."

"And that's the way it should be! But if you neglect your post, the opias will know they can sneak by you while you sleep. I'm afraid you're not taking this seriously, so I'm going to have to do something about it," the sun warned.

Macoel brushed the sun away, mocking him. The sun became angered and started to get hot with rage. Instead of calming himself down, the sun took out all his rage on Macoel, turning him into stone and giving him non-blinking eyes.[34] That way, he would never fall asleep on the job again, and the cave would be properly guarded forever. Today, of course, many lizards, including the iguana and the gecko, have eyes that appear to never blink.

The Taíno drew iguanas on the outside and inside of caves to represent the guardian Macoel.

When the Spaniards arrived on the islands, they thought the iguana was an ugly creature. It was so ugly that it could not be eaten by humans, at least in their opinion. The Taíno absolutely disagreed with this. Iguana meat was an excellent source of nourishment and was particularly delicious when barbecued or prepared in a soup (stewed with pepper). Iguanas were somewhat difficult to find and catch, making them a rare treat. The Spanish explorer Oviedo once described iguanas as "better to eat than to see," and he was just as impressed by how long the animals could survive without food. They could survive for almost twenty days!

Christopher Columbus once met a group of fishermen preparing a barbecue of smoked fish and iguana for a special feast in an area along the coast of Cuba. The Taíno people in Cuba offered to share the food with Columbus and his men but were offended when the Spaniards only ate the fish and left the iguana. They were put off by the odd look of the creature. Today, iguana is not a common source of meat in Puerto Rico and the surrounding islands due to its dwindling populations. Their presence has been diminished by years of human interference, including overeating of the original population.

In the more isolated areas of Central and South America, one can find other Indigenous cultures that are distantly related to the Taíno people. There, the iguana is still considered a vitamin-rich delicacy when eaten in soup.

The Manatee

Manatee is one of the many Taíno words that has lived on across cultures, though some call the water-dwelling mammal the sea cow. In the Taíno language, *manatí* means "breast," perhaps alluding to the similarities between the manatee mammary glands and that of a human.

The manatee is known as the sacred provider among the Taíno because it provided a life-giving source of food. The Taíno speared the

---

[34] Talking Taíno: Lizards & Snakes By William F. Keegan and Betsy Carlson
https://www.angelfire.com/va3/ritas_nativeamerican/talking-Taíno-info.html

manatee and used the meat to eat and the rest of the animal for tools and other resources, including using the ribs to carve into sculptures and purging sticks that shamans would stick down their throats to induce vomiting before cohoba rituals.[35] The belief is that purging, combined with pre-ritual fasting, would aid in communicating with the spirit world. The Taíno culture considered the manatee sacred in the same way North American Indigenous people regarded the buffalo.[36]

As a food source, manatees were very valuable, as they could offer upward of five hundred pounds of meat that kept well. The only downside was how hard it could be to hunt the mammals. A manatee could easily bump against a canoe and toss all the people aboard into the water, making hunting them dangerous.

Manatee bones were also used to make *duhos*, ceremonial seats made for only the caciques or behiques to use. They were built low to the ground and had no armrests. They look almost reminiscent of the posture inspired by the hammock (another Taíno invention). Many duhos have survived the centuries, thanks to the fact that the Taíno people hid them away in caves to avoid raiding by the Spanish.

A duho.[iv]

---

[35] Taíno Museum Article: Double Vomiting Sticks Made of Bone: https://Taínomuseum.org/portfolio-view/double-vomiting-stick-made-bone/

[36] Manatee or Manati. https://Taíno-facts.blogspot.com/2007/01/manatee-or-manati.html

How exactly manatees are featured in Taíno mythology is relatively unknown in the modern day, though the use of their bones in ritual art suggests they held a place of great importance. Bones themselves feature strongly in folklore, going back to the creation myth and the gourd of Yayael's bones that turned into the first fish released into the sea.[37]

When Columbus arrived in Puerto Rico and met the Taíno people, the manatee was one of the first animals he was shown. Having never seen the water mammal before, Columbus was confused. He first took them to be mermaids, though he was less than impressed by their look, having been told that mermaids were beautiful, seductive sirens.

The Turkey

Guanaho is the Taíno word for turkey. This is the bird that represents south on the medicine wheel. For the Taíno, the turkey represents innocence and open-mindedness. Turkeys can understand deep ideas without prejudice or preconceived notions.

Turkeys aren't native to the Antillean Islands; however, they do live on the North American continent in regions where the Taíno traded. Turkeys were present in the Maya culture and found throughout Central America and South America. They were also present in the Florida area. The fact that the Taíno included the turkey as part of their culture is direct evidence that they interacted with many other societies across the region and outside of the Taíno kingdom.[38]

As the story goes, Columbus's interactions with the Taíno people are the reason the English word for the bird is "turkey." When his interpreter saw the birds, he chose to name them *tuki*, based on a biblical description of a similar bird. From there, the word evolved into "turkey." In the Caribbean, the Taíno word *guanaho* is still used.[39]

While there is a great deal of evidence that turkeys were considered a sacred bird, they were also a rare food source for the Taíno. One of their favorite ways to prepare turkey was over the barbeque. The word

---

[37] "Taíno Zemís and Duhos (Article) | Taíno." Khan Academy - https://www.khanacademy.org/humanities/art-americas/early-cultures/xf20f462f:taino/a/taino-zemis-and-duhos

[38] Turkeys in the Caribbean https://indigenouscaribbean.ning.com/profiles/blogs/turkeys-in-the-caribbean

[39] Gilad, Elon. "A Thanksgiving Riddle: Why Are Turkeys Called Turkeys?" - https://www.haaretz.com/archaeology/2015-11-23/ty-article/.premium/why-are-turkeys-called-turkeys/0000017f-e29a-d804-ad7f-f3fa3b780000

barbeque, in fact, comes from the Taíno word *barbacoa* or *barabicu*, which translates to "sacred pit." They would dig a hole in the ground to act as a firepit and cover it with a grid of green wood that was unlikely to catch fire. Then, after starting a slow-burning fire, food such as fish, iguana, turkey, or vegetables would be laid on top.[40]

As previously mentioned, there are clues that indicate that turkeys were of religious importance to the Taíno, who believed that there were four sacred birds representing the changing seasons—spring, summer, fall, and winter—or the four cardinal directions. The four birds were the hummingbird, the red-tailed hawk, the owl, and the turkey. Though some sources refer to an eagle instead of a turkey as the fourth sacred bird, the frequent mention of the word *guanaho* proves that the intended description was that of a turkey.[41]

The Duck

The duck represents adaptability to the Taíno. The duck can go anywhere. It can fly, it can swim, and it can walk on land, making it a master of every environment because of its ability to adapt quickly to different situations. The Taíno word for duck is *yaguasa*.

As a water bird, the duck bridges the water, earth, and sky. This gives the duck a revered place in Taíno religion and culture. They are sometimes associated with the goddess Coatrisque, who is the Taíno water goddess. Any bird that can carry water from the sea to the earth while flying through the sky represents Coatrisque.[42]

The feathers of the whistling duck were also used in colorful headdresses, particularly of the Higuayagua Taíno tribe, while other feathers, like that of the owl and eagle, were reserved only for the headdresses of the behique (the shaman or medicine men).[43]

The Taíno were very adept at hunting ducks, making the bird one of their most relied-upon food sources. Columbus wrote that herds of ducks surrounded every *bohío* (the low, thatched-roofed houses of the Taíno) he saw, leading historians to wonder if ducks were also kept and

---

[40] "How the History of Caribbean Barbecue Produced the Spicy, Fruity Flavors We Know Today." https://www.foodandwine.com/cradle-of-barbecue-7550634

[41] Sague, Miguel Jr, Turkeys in the Caribbean - https://indigenouscaribbean.ning.com/profiles/blogs/turkeys-in-the-caribbean

[42] Times of the Islands – Talking Taíno: Birds of a Feather https://www.timespub.tc/2006/01/talking-Taíno-birds-of-a-feather/

[43] "Cemi and Headdress," https://www.unionhiwayawa.com/444656547.html

farmed by the Taíno.[44]

The Spanish explorer Oviedo wrote about the duck population in Puerto Rico, referring to them as stupid birds who could easily be caught by hand, leading the Spanish sailors to call them *bobos*, which was inspired by the Spanish word for clown. They were particularly easy to overpower during nesting season, and though the Spanish thought they were lackluster in terms of taste, the Taíno frequently roasted them.[45]

During seasons when the whistling ducks were more difficult to hunt, the Taíno employed clever techniques. After sending several gourds down the river, which were used in a similar way as other hunting decoys, the Taíno would go down the river themselves with gourds over their heads. When the right moment came, they would use a noose or lasso to capture the ducks by their necks.[46]

The Woodpecker

The Taíno have a significant origin myth in their culture about a woodpecker, named *inriri*, which somewhat challenges the more popular and well-known creation legend. According to the tale, the first Taíno men were anxious to find women when they emerged from the sacred cave. The first women to emerge from the cave had been kidnapped by a rogue leader, leaving the men alone.

During a heavy rain, the desperate men went out searching for any signs of women nearby. Disappointed, they weren't able to find any women on the island. Later that day, while they were bathing, the men saw something surprising in the distance. Falling from a few nearby trees, perhaps due to the storm, were some sort of human-shaped people. They ran and captured the human-like creatures, soon realizing that these people were neither male nor female.

They held the creatures captive and sought spiritual advice about how to change these creatures into the women they longed for. They were told to find a special bird named Inriri, a type of woodpecker that used its beak to make holes in the trees.

---

[44] History of the Taíno Indians. http://www.fjcollazo.com/documents/TanioIndRpt.htm

[45] Keegan, William F., and Lisabeth A. Carlson. Talking Taíno: Essays on Caribbean Natural History from a Native Perspective. - https://www.yumpu.com/en/document/read/65035176/talking-taino-caribbean-natural-history-from-a-native-perspective

[46] Farabee, William Curtis. The Central Arawaks. - https://stgeorgesinstitute.org/mycore/courses/his-301/lessons/csec-revision-3-17-01-22-theme-one-indigenous-people-and-europeans/topic/the-Ta%C3%ADno%20-arawaks/

The men took the human-like creatures, bound their hands and feet, and then led Inriri to their bodies. The bird mistook the creatures for tree trunks and began to make holes in the figures, creating an opening to the womb and giving women to the Taíno men, forever forging Inriri's place as a sacred figure.[47]

Other versions of the story say that the bodies the woodpecker transformed into women were nothing more than tree trunks. The desperate men begged Inriri to carve them into female figures. The blood from Inriri's pecking of the trees rained down on the woodpecker, creating the deep red feathers that now make the bird stand out.[48]

Another variation of the myth states that the female figures were slippery, eel-like forms possessed by evil spirits called *maboyas*. The figures would taunt the men into chasing them, even sometimes allowing themselves to be caught, before escaping at the last moment. Desperate with desire, the men asked their cacique, Guahaiona, for guidance.

Guahaiona considered the issue deeply before deciding that the only way forward was to transform the figures into proper women. Seeing as they were so hard to capture due to their slick skin, the men relied on *caracaracol* (people afflicted with scabs) to do the hunting, as they were the only men able to get a grip on the slippery creatures.[49]

Similar to other versions of the myth, the cacique and behiques performed a ritual ceremony to call upon Inriri, who they knew was skilled at carving. Inriri answered the call, but to be able to carve the women, they had to be transformed into wood. From there, Inriri got to work, creating the forms that would go on to become women.

When Inriri was done, the wooden women became real, trading their bark for skin. The evil spirits that had been controlling them were chased away by Inriri. Once they gained their humanity, women retained the knowledge of the trees they had once been, making them very gifted healers.

---

[47] From the account of Ramón Pané (1497), translated in Cave of the Jagua, Antonio M Stevens-Arroyo, University of New Mexico Press, 1988, p. 169

[48] Paralitici, Carlos, "Myth of Creation (Taíno Mythology)" - https://wsdestination.com/2020/05/05/myth-of-creation-taino-mythology/

[49] Isbani, Eli, "Notes on the Taíno Language" - https://tainolanguage.wordpress.com/2011/09/23/the-morpheme-of-k/

The myth of how women were created also bears similarities to the tales of how rainbows were first made. As discussed earlier, there is a legend of how the parrot was the one responsible for pecking a hole between the legs of a woman distracted by the beauty of the first rainbow, thereby creating the first womb. In both versions, a bird pecking at a female figure is how women were ultimately given the ability to have children.

The woodpecker is known as the spirit of artists and craftsmen for their ability to work wood and bring about transformations. The rhythmic nature of the woodpecker's pecking inspired Taíno drumming, and they even assert that Inriri was the one who first taught them how to make drums from hollowed-out logs made to look like the holes created in tree trunks by woodpeckers.

As a sacred figure, Inriri is called upon during the seeding ceremony through hand gestures that mimic the woodpecker's tapping and chants. The repeated phrases invoke Inriri by asking for an end to conflict, to end sadness, and to bless those performing the ceremony with honor.[50]

The Shark

The Taíno had several words for shark, though the most common was *kahaya*. This creature is the powerful animal of Guacar, who is known as the god of trial and error. Some also see the shark as a teacher of difficult lessons or, to use a more colloquial phrase, tough love.[51]

The *kahaya* reminds the people of the consequences of making bad choices and their ability to learn from mistakes. The *kahaya* is also the classic trickster spirit in Taíno myths and tales.[52]

Archaeologists have uncovered numerous pieces of evidence showing they used the various species of sharks surrounding the islands for economic trade. They ate the shark meat after capturing sharks when they entered the shallow waters close to shore. They utilized the teeth as spear tips and drill bits. The Taíno didn't have any metal items until the Spanish arrived and introduced metal to their culture, so bones were often used in place of iron.

---

[50] SEVEN SIRIK SEEDING CEREMONY, Caney Circle - https://caneycircle.wordpress.com/ceremonies/

[51] Sagué-Machiran, Miguel A., "Canoa: Taíno Indigenous Dream River Journey" - https://www.google.ca/books/edition/Canoa/WQXWCwAAQBAJ?hl=en&gbpv=0

[52] Animals – Caney Circle - https://caneycircle.wordpress.com/animals/

The Taíno also created decorative items from the shark's body parts. It is believed that the Taíno used cartilage from the bones; cartilage doesn't last for thousands of years, so it has long since decayed. The Taíno also made sculptures honoring the shark.[53]

Sharks and stingrays were considered deadly predators of humans. During excavations of a gravesite, archaeologists found a man missing his forearm with clear evidence of shark bite marks on the bone. Interestingly, the archaeologists also uncovered a man who had died from a stingray barb rammed into his body, lending evidence that the bones of sea creatures were utilized as weapons.[54]

To this day, shark dances are performed at solstice ceremonies in the Caribbean. The symbolic dance pits Yúcahu (god of masculinity and fertility) against Guacar, who uses a shark as his totem. The two mythological characters dance a ritualistic battle that ends with the shark getting shot, acting as a metaphor for the people's ability to overcome trials and tribulations.

Sharks appear in the mythology of other surrounding traditions. Caribbean folklore tells the stories of the Lusca, a legendary sea monster that is half-shark and half-octopus. Tales of a real animal living in the depths of the blue holes that dot the area (sinkholes surrounded by carbonite shore) have persisted into the 20th century, daring us to believe in the existence of a seventy-five-foot-long monster.[55]

Current thinking explains this creature as a legend made up by the early Caribbean peoples to warn people away from swimming near the blue holes. There is evidence to suggest that the Lusca was nothing more than a giant octopus that had the swimming style of a shark, darting around quickly to confuse those on land.[56]

---

[53] Oliver, José R. Caciques and Cemí Idols: The Web Spun by Taíno Rulers between Hispaniola and Puerto Rico.

[54] Talking Taíno: Caribbean Natural History from a Native Perspective, Ch.3, Ch. 4 https://www.everand.com/read/292064933/Talking-Taíno-Caribbean-Natural-History-from-a-Native-Perspective#__search-menu_164963

[55] Didymus, John Thomas. "Lusca." Fairy Tales and Myths - https://www.fairytalesandmyths.com/lusca/

[56] Ihearthula. "Folktale Friday: Lusca and the Blue Holes." - https://ihearthula.com/2021/03/26/folktale-friday-lusca-and-the-blue-holes/

The Turtles and Tortoises

The name for the land tortoise in the Taíno language is *jicotea*. The tortoise is said to carry the secrets of their sacred calendar on its shell. The Taíno used the pattern of scales to establish the lunar calendar. The scales circling the edge of the shell add up to twenty-eight, which matches the lunar cycle and the women's monthly cycle, adding to the turtle's reputation as a maternal figure.

The inner scales make up a geometric pattern. This pattern contains thirteen large scales that go in the center of the tortoise's shell, which matches the Maya calendar. These scales represent the thirteen perfect full moons in the lunar year, and zoomorphic representations of turtles can often be found in Taíno pottery and art. Effigy bowls were made both out of turtle shells and also in the shape of shells, often featuring fins and tails added for effect.[57]

When the first Taíno people came to inhabit the Antilles, the turtles that lived in the region were huge. Reptiles had existed in Turks and Caicos for ages without any interaction with people, and they very quickly became prey. They were brought very close to extinction within hundreds of years, though they still boasted high population numbers by the time Columbus arrived. One of the men traveling with Columbus mentioned that the ships practically ran aground on the turtles and that the sound of the shells clattering against each other could be heard on board.[58]

Turtles were a great food source for the Taíno for a long time. They were caught using nets or trapped when they were easy to catch, such as during nesting season. Turtle meat was even exported as a trading good to Haiti.

Another strange hunting method was described by the Spanish explorer Oviedo. According to his notes, the Taíno would catch remora fish and tie a rope to their tails. Remora have a suction on the bottom of their bellies that allows them to attach themselves to other kinds of fish or underwater animals. The Taíno would send the roped remora toward the turtles and reel them in once they attached themselves to the reptiles.

---

[57] Atkinson, Leslie Gail, "The Earliest Inhabitants: The Dynamics of the Jamaican Taíno." https://www.yumpu.com/en/document/read/65163424/the-earliest-inhabitants-the-dynamics-of-the-jamaican-taino

[58] Times of the Islands – Mother Sea Turtle. - https://www.timespub.tc/2008/04/mother-sea-turtle/

Do you remember Deminán from the Taíno origin myth in Chapter 1? He got a lump on his back, and from that lump sprang the turtle woman who had children with Deminán and his brothers in order to populate the earth. Other versions of the tale feature a woman appearing from Deminán's back instead of a turtle, though there are also legends that explain how women came to exist, like the one illustrated in the woodpecker's story.

Aside from the part they play in the creation myth, turtles were also venerated (like ducks) for their ability to exist both on land and in the water, leading to the idea that turtles can guide souls to the realm of the dead. For this reason, turtle shells have been found at burial sites.

Archaeologists have discovered many pieces of pottery and ritualistic tools that feature not only the turtle but also a turtle with a bird on top of it. It's been speculated that this combination of animals is meant to refer to a myth or legend that has now been forgotten.[59]

The turtle symbolizes the woman from the creation legend and the beginning of the Taíno people. The Taíno believe a turtle's back supports the American continent, as well as provides protection from evil or malevolent spirits.[60]

The Bat

The Taíno have a myth about how the bat became a naked, ugly creature of the night. It goes like this.

Early on, when time was just beginning, the bat was the ugliest creature in the world. The bat realized his own ugliness, and he flew up to heaven to find the Great Spirit. He didn't tell the Great Spirit that he felt ugly and wanted a rainbow of feathers. Instead, he pleaded.

"Please, please give me feathers for warmth. I'm freezing cold," the bat begged.

Unfortunately for the bat, the Great Spirit had no feathers left to give to the poor naked creature.

"I'll arrange for each bird to give you a feather instead," the Great Spirit told the bat.

The bat received a green parrot feather, a white dove feather, a shimmering rainbow hummingbird feather, a pink feather from a

---

[59] Doyle, James A., "Arte del Mar," Metropolitan Museum of Art Bulletin
[60] Animals – Caney Circle. https://caneycircle.wordpress.com/animals/

flamingo, and a red cardinal's feather. He also got a blue kingfisher feather, a clay-colored eagle feather, and even a beautiful sun-colored feather from the toucan.

The bat was elated. He felt as if this gorgeous assortment of feathers was the ultimate prize. He flew effortlessly between the earth and the clouds, and whenever the other birds saw him, they stared in shock and awe at his beauty. Some even say the rainbow was created from the feathered bat's flight pattern, though other stories attribute the rainbow to Yobuenahuaboshka's multi-colored threads braided high in the sky.

Before long, the bat became very vain and self-absorbed. He looked down on the other birds, thinking he was better than everyone else because of his beauty. He even went as far as to throw insults at the other birds.

The birds who had so graciously given their feathers to create the bat's beautiful suit were not going to stand for this haughty treatment. They called a meeting. They flew up to visit the Great Spirit together and informed the Great Spirit of the bat's poor behavior. They also told the Great Spirit that they were cold because of their missing feathers.

The following day, the bat was in the middle of an arching flight, feeling all of the self-confidence in the world. Suddenly, as he shook his glimmering feathers, he was horrified to see them all fall out and rain down upon the earth below.

To this day, the bat is still searching for his lost feathers. He hides and only comes out at night because he is so ashamed of his wrinkled, naked body. He hides in the caves during the day so that the other birds can't see him. He flies erratically and quickly, never stopping, as he is unwilling to risk the other birds catching a glimpse of him.[61]

This myth is reminiscent of the story of how the owl became nocturnal, hiding in the dark to keep the other birds from stealing their feathers back. Like the owl, the bat is considered a symbol of the dead. The Taíno believed that because bats lived in caves and only came out at night, they carried the souls of the recently dead. As a result, the Taíno invited them to feast on guavas until the sun threatened to send them back into the cave.

Both the bat and the owl are connected to the cemí responsible for the realm of the dead, Maquetaurie Guayaba, whose caves they often

---

[61] Taíno Legends. https://www.indigenouspeople.net/tainmyth.htm

inhabit. It's been theorized that bats were connected to *opias* (spirits of the dead) because of their similarities to humans. Both are mammals that feed one child at a time, but they can also take flight, which is something only humans are capable of once they become an *opia*.

This ability to transition and cross borders between worlds fascinated the Taíno, and it helped to explain the importance of certain animals in their mythology. Bats exist and thrive in both caves and the sky, while ducks and turtles have the unique ability to live in water and on land. Manatees similarly share the unique characteristics of mammals while being able to breathe underwater.[62]

In the creation myth, Maquetaurie Guayaba's cave, where all Taíno came from and where the spirits go after death in the form of bats and owls, acts as a stand-in for a womb. As such, some experts wonder if the Taíno hoped and believed *opias* living in bat form were growing their strength in the womb-like cave, only to be rebirthed when ready. This is in keeping with the belief that bats and owls could carry the spirits both in and out of their caves.

The Taíno not only believed that the bats carrying the *opias* would come out at night to eat guava but also that the bats could turn into fruit themselves, representing the cyclical nature of life and death.[63]

The bat features in many mythologies and folklore around the world. The animal is often associated with death and dark matters of the underworld, like the vampire bats of eastern Europe.

Closer to the realm of the Taíno, the Toba of northern Argentina tell stories of a bat-like hero who originally taught people the ways of life, while in Brazil, the Ge tribe believes bats can lead people to the light. The Maya worshiped a god named Camazotz, a vampire bat who would kill and escort dying men to the underworld, taking on a similar position as the bat in Taíno mythology.[64]

---

[62] Keegan, William F., and Lisabeth A. Carlson. Talking Taíno: Essays on Caribbean Natural History from a Native Perspective.

[63] Poviones-Bishop, Maria, "The Bat and The Guava - Life and Death in The Taíno Worldview" - https://www.scribd.com/document/200707115/The-Bat-and-the-Guava-Life-and-Death-in-the-Taino-Worldview-By-Maria-Poviones-Bishop

[64] Mikkola, Heimo, editor. Bats - Disease-Prone but Beneficial. - https://www.intechopen.com/chapters/80107

The Jaguar

Jaguars do not and have never lived on the Caribbean islands. On this, the experts can agree, but it doesn't explain why jaguar symbology persists in the Taíno culture.

Archaeologists have found jaguar teeth with holes drilled in them to create pendants on the Caribbean islands, though they predate the Taíno people, originating with the Saladoids (ancestors of the Taíno). Jaguar teeth aren't the only non-native animal remains that have been found in the area (turkeys were also brought and traded on the islands), though the jaguar is the only one of those animals that appears to be of spiritual significance.

In addition to the limited genuine jaguar teeth found on the islands, effigies of jaguar teeth have been discovered. These were made out of more easily accessible materials, such as manatee bone. The detailed work that went into carving these replicas of jaguar teeth serves as evidence that the Taíno held an affinity for these objects, if not the animal itself, which might have only been seen by their ancestors hundreds of years earlier after they first arrived on the islands from South America.[65]

In the Taíno religion, it was believed that behiques could transform into jaguars, which allowed them to be able to meditate on the space between good and evil. There are some scholars who believe the reverence that the Taíno had for the jaguar based on their ancestors' traditions morphed over the years, with the jaguar eventually being replaced with the dog, which was a more common animal in the area.[66]

The Dog

We know that the Taíno people held dogs in high regard, as evidenced by the cemí Opiyelguabirán, a dog-like god who helps to guard the entrance to the afterlife or guide spirits there, depending on the story.

Aside from the cemí dog, which is sometimes compared to Cerberus, the Taíno also domesticated dogs as pets. Alcos or Josibi, the breed of dog native to the Caribbean islands, is now extinct, but they were known for their kind nature and lack of bark. There is some evidence that the

---

[65] Sague, Miguel Jr., "Jaguars in the Caribbean?" https://indigenouscaribbean.ning.com/profiles/blogs/jaguars-in-the-caribbean.

[66] Keegan, William F. Taíno Indian Myth and Practice: The Arrival of the Stranger King.

Taíno used the dogs to help when hunting hutia, but that information is limited.[67]

It's hard to say which animal the Taíno preferred as a domesticated pet: the dog or the parrot. The writings of the European colonizers show that the Spanish were fascinated with the mute dogs of the Taíno, which were very different from their loud Greyhounds.

In 1519, the famed cacique Enriquillo, who had been educated and converted by the Spanish, reunited with his people to form a rebellion. Legend has it he fought using Spanish dogs. Enriquillo made sure to keep the dogs apart from the rest of his people, knowing that if the Spanish heard the barking, they would be giving up the dogs' location.

Though he wasn't able to force the Spanish out, Enriquillo is still hailed as a hero and celebrated with statues to this day. Some say Enriquillo was the last pure Taíno in the Dominican Republic, assuming that no one survived the Spanish conquests or disease, though current thinking and research say that the Taíno people and culture live on in a multitude of ways.[68]

Dogs make appearances in many different mythological traditions around the world. One of the most infamous ways that dogs show up in legend is the dog-headed people known as the Cynocephali. The Cynocephali were worshiped as gods in some places, and they were known to many cultures around the world, from ancient Greece to India and Egypt.

Columbus claimed after his meetings with the Taíno people that they were aware of the existence of the Cynocephali, though it is unclear whether or not they had encountered any themselves or merely heard stories and seen representations of the human-dog hybrids.

Mythological Hybrid Animals

As has been mentioned throughout our exploration of animals in Taíno mythology, there are several occurrences of hybrid animals, like the Lusca (a half-shark, half-octopus creature), the Cynocephali (half-dog, half-human), and Iguanaboína, the god formed from a snake and iguana, though they are not the only three examples.

---

[67] Wagschal, Steven. Minding Animals In The Old And New Worlds: A Cognitive Historical Analysis.

[68] Guitar, Lynne, "Documenting the Myth of Taíno Extinction."
https://ia800206.us.archive.org/3/items/KacikeJournal/GuitarEnglish.pdf

La Ciguapa is perhaps the most frightening illustration of mythological creatures believed to be real or known to the Taíno people. While evidence of La Ciguapa is not found in any cave paintings or pieces of art discovered by archaeologists, the Taíno people of the Dominican Republic claim the story. She takes a human form, though her skin is sometimes described as blue. Her long, luxurious hair covers her naked body. Her hair reaches all the way down to her feet, which face backward.

Men are warned to stay far, far away from La Ciguapa while they work in the fields or forests, lest they fall prey to her bird-like calls and emotional moans. Rumor has it that if she catches you, she will consume you slowly and entirely. She sucks her victims' blood and leaves nothing but dried bones.[69]

La Ciguapa is not the only siren-like creature associated with the Taíno culture. There are several interpretations of how the mermaid Aycayia came to be, but in all the versions, she was a beautiful woman with several talents, including dancing.

It is said that Aycayia was one of the only surviving dancers from a terrible boat accident in her village. After the accident, Aycayia was seen by the other women to be hogging all the attention of their husbands, luring them away from their duties and homes.

Eventually, the cacique exiled Aycayia to a faraway island, but even there, the men could still hear her sweet song. Some of them followed her, seduced by the notion of seeing out their days with her on their own island. Fed up, the cacique and behiques consulted the cemís, who vowed to take care of the problem.

The gods decided to turn Aycayia into a mermaid, a half-human, half-fish creature destined to live the rest of her life in the ocean. Some versions say that she lived with an old woman, who was also turned into a turtle by the cemís, and yet another version says that Aycayia rides this turtle across the ocean waves. From time to time, Aycayia refers to a group of women instead of a single dancer, all of whom were banished. They attempt to seduce men from their place of exile.[70]

---

[69] Vínculo, Obtener, et al. La Ciguapa – The Woman with Backwards Feet. https://www.artisticord.com/2013/09/la-ciguapa-dominican-succubus.html

[70] Muir, Evie. "Black Mermaid Folklore Has Been Around Long Before Disney's The Little Mermaid." - https://www.wbur.org/hereandnow/2022/09/30/black-mermaids-the-little-disney

All these versions of Aycayia are reminiscent of other mermaid tales, and the Taíno siren's story is still being adapted to this day. In Monique Roffey's 2022 reimagining of Aycayia in *The Mermaid of Black Conch*, she was initially ostracized because she refused to get married and then became a source of fascination for the local men. The jealous wives confined half of her in a fish's tail, condemning her to the sea. A thousand years later, in 1976, Aycayia falls in love with a local fisherman.

The legend of Maitio and Iasiga is another Taíno story that involves a traitorous woman being exiled to the sea and transformed into an unrecognizable creature. In the beginning, Maitio and Iasiga were a happily married Ciboney (the Taíno of Jamaica and central Cuba) couple.

At least they were happy before Iasiga laid eyes on Gaguiano, another Ciboney man, as he picked fruit from the garden. He was so handsome, and their connection was so instantaneous that their love could not be denied.

Their affair started quickly, and though Iasiga truly loved her husband, she and Gaguiano needed each other in a way she hadn't experienced before. Though Maitio was a trusting man, he started to notice his wife's increasing absence. One day, when he came home to find her missing, he asked the neighbors if they knew where she was.

The neighbors were positive that Iasiga had gone to visit the graves of her ancestors because they'd seen her pass by with a basket of fruit. Full of suspicion, Maitio jumped in his canoe and paddled over to where his wife's ancestors were buried. Sure enough, he saw her there, but she wasn't alone.

Iasiga and Gaguiano were caught in an embrace. When Iasiga caught sight of her husband, she let out a cry of sorrow, knowing that everything was about to change. The cowardly Gaguiano ran off, but Iasiga stayed to meet her husband, who approached slowly and angrily. Then, Maitio prayed to the gods, pleading with them to punish his wayward wife.

The gods answered his call, swiftly turning Iasiga into a sea monster. The legends don't tell us what Iasiga looked like in her sea monster form, but it is said that her spirit is in the manatees that come close to shore, appearing mute and helpless to the fishermen who paddle close. Elements of this story are similar to those found in early Cuban folklore of the Siboney people.[71]

---

[71] La India Maldita en tradiciones y leyendas de Cienfuegos. https://cubamemorias.com/la-india-maldita-en-tradiciones-y-leyendas-de-cienfuegos/

The themes of seductive, untrustworthy women meeting a fate determined by cemís or gods appear frequently in Taíno mythology, though we know that women were also worshiped and honored since the Taíno tracked their heritage through matrilineal lines.

Chapter 4: Cohoba Rituals and Sacred Ceremonies

In Taíno culture, behiques were shamans who communicated with the spirit world to gather wisdom for their people. In order to leave the human realm and access the spirit world, the behiques snuffed a powdered substance called cohoba.

Cohoba is a hallucinogen made from the ground seeds of the *Anadenanthera peregrina* tree. This tree grows natively on the Caribbean islands. Sometimes, powdered tobacco was mixed with the cohoba powder, along with red and brown ground herbs and smoked crushed snail shells.

Friar Ramón Pané, who arrived on the Antillean Islands with Columbus, described the cohoba ritual in detail from his experiences while living among the Taíno. After snorting the powder, its psychoactive effects took over quickly. The person will quickly lose consciousness, and their arms and legs will droop. Suddenly, the person will begin to talk of the room spinning and things moving around in otherworldly ways. The visions the behiques experienced influenced their decisions on important political matters, such as tribal disputes or making judgments. They used the visions to predict the yield of crops and even when planning war. The behiques also believed that, as shamans, they could use cohoba to help them gain wisdom and power in order to cure an ill member of the village.

Caves, which the Taíno regarded as sacred in their culture, contain art from visions experienced by behiques during cohoba ceremonies.

When did the Taíno hold cohoba ceremonies? Archaeological evidence and the notes written by Friar Ramón Pané have led historians to believe that cohoba was used frequently. It could have been taken during community gatherings, for a ceremony celebrating a rite of passage, for a religious event, and to mark the death of a person in the village.

Friar Ramón Pané gives extra detail about one situation where a behique utilized cohoba. In his writings, Pané explains that the behique contacted a spirit or ancestor to ask for the spirit to identify itself and reveal its powers. The example given by Pané is of a spirit revealing itself in a tree to the behique by "moving its roots and speaking."

The behique then used cohoba powder to ask the tree how it would like to be used. Would it like to become a cemí? A house? Something different?

The tree would get its wish, being made into whatever the tree's spirit requested. They would continue to honor that spirit by taking cohoba for it.

Who participated in the cohoba rituals? The rituals were primarily led by the behiques of each village since their job as shamans was to connect with the spiritual realm. At times, they were joined by important members of the community. Caciques, who were the community leaders, often took part in the ceremony to communicate with *zemis*, the spirits and ancestors.

What steps were involved in the cohoba ceremony? The ceremonies typically took place in the house of the village chief, or the cacique. Christopher Columbus noted that the cohoba ceremonies he witnessed often took place in an empty house with a large room containing nothing but cohoba paraphernalia. Columbus described the location as comparable to a church because it was seen as a sacred space solely for ceremonial use.[72]

Prior to beginning the ceremony, the participants would paint their bodies. Next, they would purify themselves by using vomiting spatulas to purge the contents of their stomachs. The vomiting spatula was made of

---

[72] Times of the Islands – Partying, Taíno -style https://www.timespub.tc/2007/06/partying-Taíno-style/

either carved wood or a manatee rib and decorated with the figures of gods and goddesses or important animals. Columbus described these vomiting spatulas as being up to fifty centimeters long. That's nearly twenty inches in length!

A purging spatula.˅

As the participants entered the room, they were greeted by the cacique or behique, who would be playing a wooden drum called the *bayohabao or mayohucán*.⁷³ He would be seated on the *duho*, a special ceremonial seat. The duho was typically carved from a heavy, dark wood that was inlaid with gold and shells. Only the community leaders or spiritual leaders were allowed to sit on this bench. It was brought out during ceremonies and community events. From the duho, the leaders communicated with the spiritual realm and transferred their wisdom to the community.

---

⁷³ Ritual Taíno de la Cohoba. https://pueblosoriginarios.com/centro/antillas/Taíno /cohoba.html

In the center of the room sat a *cemí*. The cemí is a sacred carving that represents a god, goddess, or ancestral spirit. These would be anthropomorphic and zoomorphic figures representing humans or animals. The carvings were primarily made from wood, but at times, they could have been carved from stone or another material. The cemí was believed to hold the spiritual power of the spirit they represented. The cemí chosen for each ritual would be the one that the behique planned on consulting during the ceremony.[74]

Cemís were idols that served as an intermediary between the physical and spiritual realms. Emerging from the cemí's head or back was a platform, on the top of which was placed a shiny black platter with a dip in the center, likely carved from stone. Cohoba powder would be placed on this platter.

The powder was snorted through the nose using a hollow wooden tube, often a reed, that was reworked to be Y-shaped on the end to allow for both nostrils to inhale the powder at the same time. The snuff tubes have been aptly referred to as conduits to the supernatural.

After the powder was inhaled, the participants immediately became high and disoriented, going limp and then reportedly seeing everything in a mirror image or reverse. Men walked backward, for example, and every movement or gesture was seen as happening in reverse. The world was filled with intense colors that shifted; it was as if their eyes had become kaleidoscopes. While under the influence of cohoba, the world was inverse from reality. This led the behiques to believe they were able to see past the mortal realm and directly view the fibers and tissues of the universe, giving them access to every realm so that they could communicate with the gods and ancestor spirits.

For the Taíno, the natural hallucinogens they ground into powder were considered very sacred because they gave the behiques the force of the universe in the palm of their hand. From the Europeans' viewpoint, the use of hallucinogenic plants did not allow the native Taíno people to access anything sacred. In fact, the Europeans judged the Indigenous ceremonies of all cultures they interacted with, including the ayahuasca and peyote hallucinogens of North American and South American tribes.

---

[74] Times of the Islands – Partying, Taíno-style. https://www.timespub.tc/2007/06/partying-Taíno-style/

The Christian European worldview had the Spaniards convinced that the Taíno were communicating directly with the devil. This negative perception caused a cascade of interventions from the Spaniards as they conquered the Indigenous peoples of the Americas.

Missionaries referred to peyote, ayahuasca, and cohoba as "satanic trickery" or "diabolic brews."[75] They looked down on the tribes for their uncivilized behavior when they witnessed the cohoba ceremony and considered them a people in need of the Catholic religion. They had no respect for the Taíno people and their vastly different worldview.

As the Europeans conquered the Taíno and other Indigenous cultures, they quickly outlawed these "evil" hallucinogenic substances, even though they were derived from naturally growing plants native to each people group's respective geographical location. Effectively, the Europeans forbade the Taíno and other Indigenous people from practicing their religion. This criminalization and negative perception of plant-based hallucinogenic substances still persists across North America today.

The simple fact that many Indigenous cultures across the Americas had similar ceremonies involving hallucinogenic plant-based substances that allowed them to communicate with the spirit world hints at a cohesiveness that transcends location and culture. The Indigenous people shared a worldview that believed there was a hidden spiritual aspect in everything that exists on the earth. Everything was intimately related, both the seen and the unseen. They believed the nature we can see had a strong relationship with the intelligent forces we cannot see with our human eyes. Cohoba, ayahuasca, and peyote allowed them to see what is normally unseen and to find the perfect balance between the realms.

Some scholars have noted that without taking a trip to the altered dimension of consciousness that many Indigenous tribes used as the basis of their spiritual beliefs, complete knowledge and deep understanding of Indigenous cultures is not possible.

---

[75] Indigenous and Mestizo Use of Ayahuasca: An Overview. https://kodu.ut.ee/~hellex/aya/kirjandus/kultuur/Indigenous_and_Mestizo_Use_of_Ayahuasca.pdf

Chapter 5: The Cemís: Symbols and Idols in Taíno Culture

The Taíno people that Columbus encountered lived in a world where supernatural beings ruled everything. They were immersed in their religion and myths and had no major interference or influence from other cultures to change their ways. The only other people the Taíno interacted with were also Indigenous cultures with similar worldviews, though they had slightly different beliefs and cultures from their own. The Christian worldview was entirely foreign and unfamiliar to the Taínos.

When the Catholic Spaniards and Portuguese met the Taíno, they immediately judged their religious ceremonies as being from the devil, noting their idol worship of stone and wood statues. Friar Pané, who came with Columbus and studied the Taíno people, noted that the Taínos would run into the woods and hide their most precious cemís from the European Christians for fear that they would take them.

These idols were central to the Taíno belief system. They were an integral part of daily life and also incredibly sacred to the people.

The Taíno called their statues cemís or zemis. These small statues linked together the mythical past, filled with supernatural creation stories and the power of gods and goddesses, to the present-day people. Cemís acted as a sort of bridge between the ancestral deities and the cacique who ruled over each village. Taínos believed that the objects themselves housed the spirit or deity they represented.

There are several possible spellings of cemís. Singular could be cemí, cimi, or zemi, and the plural form includes zemis. The word "cemí" itself in the Taíno language does not refer to the object. Instead, a cemí is an immaterial thing, a vital force, and an invisible power that is represented in the spirit of the stone or wood representation.

In addition to representing deities, a cemí could also represent the spirits of dead ancestors. Since the Taíno organized their societal structure into chiefdoms, they also developed communal deities that represented each village or belonged to each caique. Cemís could be male or female.

The highest-ranking caciques owned the most powerful cemís. The cacique held both the social power and religious power in village life, so it was only natural they would also be in control of the cemís. Other caciques would attempt to steal these cemís away.

The cohoba ritual allowed the cacique or behique to enter a trance-like state and communicate with the cemí. The messages the cacique received could have been advice, wisdom, or answers to questions like how to handle a military conquest or how to solve medical problems.

The messages from the cemí were seen as divine orders, as communication straight from the mythical spirit world. Since these messages could be delivered directly to the cacique, they helped him keep his power in the village by earning him the ultimate respect.

The residents of the village would honor the cemís by giving offerings from their harvests or fasting for a long time in their honor, and they would pay homage to the cemí during a cohoba ceremony. These offerings were seen as repayments for the gifts and wisdom with which the spirit of the cemí had blessed the cacique. In turn, this continued to reaffirm the power of the cacique in the eyes of the people.

In addition to communal village cemís, there were also family and individual cemís. The caciques of most villages had three stone cemís. They represented important things that were vital to living a good life in a Taíno village. The first cemí was for a good grain and vegetable harvest. The second cemí was for helping women give birth safely and without extreme pain. The third stone cemí was for the blessings of water and sun.

The stones would be kept wrapped in cotton and carried in small baskets. The people would feed or offer them whatever foods they were eating. According to Friar Pané, the Taínos treated cemís in their homes in the same manner.

Friar Pané also noted that women collected small stones that remained uncarved but were treated in the same manner as cemís. There was a possibility, according to Friar Pané, that the three stones being collected were three kinds of cemís taken from the bodies of sick people by the priests and doctors to be used in healing rituals.

Cemís carved of wood had a unique creation story, which we mentioned briefly in the previous chapter about cohoba ceremonies. The tree would be seen moving its roots about, and a behique would be summoned to perform a cohoba ceremony to communicate with the spirit and ask who it was, what it wished for, what it was doing there, and what powers it possessed. The new cemí would then be carved out of the tree's wood.

One kind of cemí would contain the bones of family members and ancestors. These cemís were always made of stone or wood. They were created to be full-bodied statues. They were always wrapped in cotton or placed in a bowl made from the calabash.

The ancestor cemís were always linked to a surviving relative. The cemís have an entire web of familial relationships from idol to idol and through living human relatives. With these cemís, there were two relationships for family members. The first relationship was between an ancestral cemí and the caretaker. The living human was required to bring the cemí food and goods or perform favors. The second type of relationship was that of kinship. That was an obligatory relationship similar to one between cousins, uncles, aunts, or husbands and wives.[76]

There are a handful of well-documented cemís that we still have information about today despite the limited history left behind by the Taínos.

Baibrama

This cemí is related to the domestication of a vital crop to the Taínos: yucca (also known as cassava or manioc). This cemí could cause disease or sickness to the people who didn't give food to the family in charge of caring for the cemí.

There's a story behind Baibrama. During wartime, the cemí got burned. The people squeezed the liquid from the yucca to wash the cemí, and before long, the body, eyes, and arms of the Baibrama cemí regenerated.

---

[76] Caciques and Cemi Idols by José R. Oliver - https://www.ubcpress.ca/caciques-and-cemi-idols

Baraguabel

Baraguabel was carved from a tree trunk that came to life. The cemí belonged to the famous cacique Guarionex and is known as a slippery cemí. Even when the people tied it up, it still managed to escape and return to the original place it was moved from. Scholars have linked Baraguabel to the ocean.

Corocote

Corocote belonged to the cacique named Guamorete. The Taínos believed this cemí had relations with women during the night. Corocote wore two crowns on its head. This cemí was also a slippery one, as it was able to return back to the place where it was taken from. Once, when its place of worship caught on fire, the cemí moved itself to a lake or river that was nearby.

Márohu

This small stone cemí is the twin to Boinayel. They are both sons of the Great Serpent. Márohu is part of the group of gods that rule over the weather. Márohu is in charge of the clear skies and is also linked to the sun. It is also known as the Spirit of the Clear Time or God of the Clear Weather.

Opiyelguabirán

This wooden cemí had four legs, similar to a dog, and belonged to the cacique Sabananiobabo. Opiyelguabirán was the third slippery cemí, as it was able to escape even when tied up, preferring to escape into the forest. As mentioned in the chapter exploring the gods, Opiyelguabirán fled when it saw the Spaniards arrive, hiding deep in the water of a nearby lagoon. No one ever saw the Opiyelguabirán cemí again.

The Balance of the Weather

In a place called Iguanaboína, known as the Region of the Dawn, there was a cave where the Taínos kept two twin male cemís. They were Boinayel, the God of Rain, and Márohu, the Spirit of the Clear Time.

The Taínos had a ritual they performed to keep the weather balanced. When it didn't rain, the hands of Boinayel would be untied. When it was raining too much, they would tie Boinayel's hands and untie the hands of Márohu. The Taíno believed that the cemís could control the sun, the moon, the night, and the day, as well as the rain and drought.

Iguanaboína, who was known as the Great Serpent Mother and the mother of Boinayel and Márohu, formed a triad with her twin sons that kept the balance of the weather intact. If an imbalance of the weather occurred and nature got out of control, that was the fault of Guabancex, who formed a triad with two male cemís— Guataubá, the bringer of bad weather, and Coatrisque, who corralled the waters and created floods. Guabancex was the complete opposite of the peaceful Iguanaboína. One trio of gods represented destruction, while the other trio represented harmonization.

The Taíno weather gods, goddesses, and myths seem to mirror the beliefs of the South American Indigenous cultures, such as the Inca and Tukanoan people. Both cultures base their myths on the three constellations in the night sky: Scorpio, Sagittarius, and Capricorn.[77]

---

[77] *The Mythology and Religion of the Taínos* by Sebastián Robiou-Lamarche.

Chapter 6: The Myth of Guabancex: The Taíno Storm Goddess

She can make the sky swirl with dark clouds and bring strong winds down to ruin crops, flood fields, or bring impossibly tall trees to the ground. Guabancex, the goddess of storms, destruction, and mayhem, was nothing like the other gods. The myths say that she is a dark manifestation of Atabey, one of the two supreme gods or ancestral spirits of the Taíno people.

Why exactly Atabey was brought to such a place of anger and chaos as to create and embody her dangerous alter ego, Guabancex, is unknown. Perhaps she was manifested out of madness and grief when her son, Yayael, attempted to kill his father, Yaya. Whatever the reason, the world was never the same once Guabancex began wielding her strength, doing her best to destroy the Antilles.

In her cemí form, Guabancex often appears with swirling arms, imitating the form of cataclysmic winds, hurricanes, and tornadoes. This detail is quite significant, indicating that the Taíno had an intimate knowledge of the form that hurricanes could take, complete with the eye of the storm, a fact that would not be discovered by Western scientists for hundreds of years.

Considering how dangerous Guabancex could be, there was only one being who could be entrusted with keeping her happy and preventing the kinds of storms she was capable of producing. Aumatex, a local cacique who ruled over the land, was charged with watching over Guabancex. Thanks to his position, he was sometimes referred to as a god of wind for his abilities to appease Guabancex.

He did his best to keep her content, showing constant attention to her through sacrifice, rituals, and ceremonial offerings. From what we know of the Taíno traditions, such offerings might have included gourds stuffed with fruit or filled with water, beautifully painted pottery, baskets, and other pieces of craftwork.

Princess Guanina

Legends such as the tale of the Taíno Princess Guanina seem to confirm the possibility of human sacrifice to appease the cemís. As the story goes, Guanina had fallen desperately in love with a Spanish soldier by the name of Don Cristobal de Sotomayor. She had acted as his guide in the area when he'd first arrived, and though he did not speak her language and she spoke only a little of his, Guanina was infatuated with the tall, handsome Spaniard.

Through their time together, they grew close, as she shared what she could of her culture with him. As the weeks went by, however, Guanina's brother started to grow suspicious. He hated the Spanish for everything they were doing to the Taíno people. He would never be able to find it in himself to forgive them. Tensions grew worse between the Taíno and the Spanish until Guanina was forbidden from seeing her lover ever again.

Of course, the princess was too in love to ever give up on Cristobal. Perhaps she snuck out late at night to see him at the Spanish fort so they could plan their escape together.

"Please don't do anything to hurt him," Guanina begged once her brother, Guaybana, found out what was going on between his sister and the Spanish captain.

"After what he and his people have done to us and this land, revenge is the only option," the angry Guaybana responded. "And don't even think about warning him. I'm not going to let you out of my sight."

Cristobal's soldiers tried to warn him to be careful, telling him that it would be best to stay in the fort until the threat had been subdued. Even Guanina pleaded with him to be careful because she knew just how strong her brother's stubbornness was. If he said he wanted to kill Cristobal, then there was practically nothing that would stop him.

However, Cristobal was not going to be frightened by rumors of one man's vendetta. He had plans to travel to the capital, Caparra. In fact, so brazenly stubborn was Cristobal that he insisted Guaybana, of all people, be summoned to help carry his baggage.

Of course, Guaybana followed through with his plan for assassination. He and his men attacked Cristobal's faction, taking them down easily, thanks to the Spaniard's unwillingness to take the necessary precautions.

Guanina was devastated. She ran to the site of the murder as soon as she could, kissing her dead lover over and over again in the hopes that it would bring him back to life. Alas, it was not to be.

Ashamed to hear of the princess's act of treason and betrayal, the Taínos decided that she was to be sacrificed to the cemís. Guaybana's small revolution had gone off just as planned without a single Taíno casualty. That was a blessing that the cemís needed to be thanked for, especially Guabancex, seeing as the storm season was nearing.

When they found her, however, Guanina was already dead, lying on her lover's dead body, tears dried on her cheeks. In the end, Guaybana decided they should be buried together under the branches of a ceiba tree. They say that if the conditions are just right and sweet nothings are whispered on a clear night, Guanina's and Cristobal's spirits can be seen looking up at the stars.

Whether Guabancex would have been pleased with the sacrifice of Princess Guanina is uncertain, but there were certainly plenty of times when no amount of gifts from Aumatex could protect the realm, even with help from neighboring caciques who came with offerings of food for the wayward and aggressive cemí. Aumatex even earned himself the title of "Chief of the Wind" and is since remembered as a god of wind, though he was no more in control of Guabancex's emotions than she was.

Guabancex's Storms

Guabancex certainly didn't act alone when she swooped her arms around, picking up wind and water until destruction could be guaranteed. The cemí retained two assistants named Coatrisque and Guataubá. The former was charged with ordering and threatening all the other cemís until they agreed to gather the strongest winds they could. Guataubá whipped up the rain and ocean water until the land itself was almost submerged.

During the summer months, Guabancex and her storms raged the hardest, making travel and farming increasingly difficult. It was for this reason that the Taíno people developed strategic farming techniques to minimize the effects of high winds. Crops with deep roots could withstand the most damage, resulting in a reliance on food such as yautia (a root crop with tough skin), taro, and yucca.

The Taíno also built their homes with the intent of minimizing damage from Guabancex's storms. The bohios they designed were constructed low to the ground and topped with thatched roofs to help give solid shelter, unlike the houses the Spanish built for themselves. The wisdom and storm-prepping traditions of the Taíno were carried on throughout the centuries, even to the slaves and their owners who went on to live in the area.

When the storms subsided in the winter months, the door was open for raiding populations to attack. The Caribs from farther south often traveled north to raid for food and women to take captive.[78]

Guabancex's Legacy

The legacy of Guabancex is a familiar one, as it is reminiscent of other Mother Nature figures that are capable of giving life and taking it in violent, horrific ways. Another deity that Guabancex is often compared to is the Hindu goddess Kali, sometimes referred to as "She Who is Death." Kali, like Guabancex, is associated with powers of both death and motherly love, reminding us of the being that Guabancex sprang from: the all-powerful mother of the Taíno, Atabey.

Like Guabancex, Kali was also born of another god. Parvati, the goddess of abundance and fertility, was sent to defeat evil demons and spirits. While in battle, however, a darker part of her was ignited, angered by the cruel spirits. Matching their barbarous ways, Parvati became something and someone else entirely, morphing into Kali. In her new form, Kali was able to decapitate her demon foes without a second thought, explaining the frequent depictions of her with weapons, skulls, and bloody lips.[79]

---

[78] "Chapter 1. Storms and Gods in a Spanish Sea." *Sea of Storms: A History of Hurricanes in the Greater Caribbean from Columbus to Katrina.* https://muse.jhu.edu/book/36465/

[79] Sague, Miguel Jr., "The Identity of Guabancex, Spirit of Natural Disasters." https://indigenouscaribbean.ning.com/profiles/blogs/the-identity-of-guabancex-spirit-of-natural-disasters

Kali is not the only deity with similarities to Guabancex. In Greek mythology, Eris (sister to Ares, the god of war and courage) represents strife and discord. The best example of the role she plays can be found in the story of the Trojan War, which Eris is often blamed for, though she never sided with either the Trojans or the Greeks.

As the story goes, Eris was feeling vengeful after being excluded from the wedding of Peleus and Thetis, so she decided to stir the pot by challenging the goddesses Athena, Aphrodite, and Hera to name who amongst them was the fairest. In the end, the task was passed on to Paris, who named Aphrodite as the fairest after she promised him the hand of Helen of Troy. The fact that Helen was already married started the war that legends are built on. It was a war that Eris supposedly watched from the sidelines with violent glee. Though Guabancex likely would never have been so content to simply be an audience to destruction, she and Eris share many similarities in their affinity for discord.[80]

While there isn't a direct comparison for Guabancex in Norse mythology, t both Thor and Loki share similarities. War is just one of Thor's many specialties, but he is known for his ruthlessness and his command of the elements, just as is Guabancex. Thor's name directly translates to "thunder," and his famous hammer, Mjölnir, means "lightning."[81]

The Taíno believed that a storm signified that Guabancex was displeased or had grown angry with them, perhaps because of a lack of attention. Similarly, when the ancient Norse people saw the sky brighten with lightning, followed by a crack of thunder, it was believed that the god Thor was brimming with rage. His hammer brought fire down to the earth, but up above the clouds, Thor might have been using it in battle to defend his realm against rival gods.

One of the main differences between Guabancex and Thor seems to boil down to their intentions. While Thor represents everything that is honorable and courageous in the world, the storms that Guabancex summoned amidst her anger were fueled by pure destruction.

There is another Norse god who was particularly attracted to creating mayhem around them. Loki, like Kali, Guabancex, and Eris, has a special affinity for causing distress and disruption. Chaos is how Loki

---

[80] Miate, Liana. "Eris." https://www.worldhistory.org/Eris/
[81] "Thor." Norse Mythology for Smart People. https://norse-mythology.org/

gains control, as illustrated by his reputation as a trickster. His form of destruction is bound in cleverness, like in the story of how he killed the god Baldur.

Thanks to a prophecy foretelling Baldur's death, the gods were able to take precautions to protect him from everything but mistletoe. Not to be dissuaded, Loki slips into a disguise and makes a spear from mistletoe, killing Baldur. Despite pleas from the other gods, Baldur is not released from the underworld, and there's only Loki to blame.[82]

Today, we remember Guabancex through the hurricanes that still swirl through the Antilles. Some say that by remembering the Taíno culture, Guabancex can be kept at bay. The Taíno farming techniques carry on to this day as well, which were developed to better survive Guabancex's wrath.

---

[82] Socotra, Vic, The Goddess of Storms. https://www.vicsocotra.com/wordpress/2016/06/13144/

Chapter 7: Life, Death, and Afterlife: Taíno Beliefs and Legends

The Taíno people had various myths based around caves. A cave was where all the Taíno people first emerged, and it was also where their spirits were carried off to die or linger in the bodies of owls and bats before finally being admitted into the land of the dead: Coaybay.

Coaybay was described to Spanish explorers at the time as a faraway and inaccessible area on the other side of the island. It was ruled by the god Maquetaurie Guayaba. Though it is the land of the dead, Coaybay was not known to be a horrible, hell-like place but instead a land where the dead spirits could enjoy the same pleasures as the living.

The Taíno believed that the spirits of the dead were called *opias*, while the spirits of the living were called *goeiza*. The opias were capable of great trickery, taking the form of recognizable people, animals (bats or owls), or even fruit.

When the opias take human form, it can be very difficult to tell the difference between them and the living, or goeiza. One clue is to look at the navel of the spirit. Opias were believed not to have navels at all, as the navel represents the connection between a mother and child. Without a navel, a spirit must not have experienced a human life.

For the Taíno, death did not necessarily mean the end. The spirits of the dead had simply been transported to Coaybay, to some unreachable part of the island. When the sun came down, then they could travel back to the land of the living to frolic, enjoy fruits, and maybe even have sex with the living.

Death Rituals

There are conflicting accounts of how the Taíno honored their dead. The ancestors of the Taíno, the Saladoid people, were known to bury their dead in the predecessors of the batey courts or in other public places that had spiritual meaning. Archaeological evidence shows that the Taíno culture became more individualistic than the Saladoid people, illustrated by how they buried their dead closer to home or even under the floors.

Caves were also frequently used as interment grounds, decorated with pictures of spirits. Higher-ranking Taíno people, such as caciques, were buried or interred amongst their most loved material possessions. There are stories of living wives being buried with great caciques.

Though little is known of any death rites, there is evidence that the Taíno people cremated their dead before burying the remains in or around caves. In the case where any bones might not have been completely burned, the bones were sometimes covered in clay and placed in decorative gourds to be hung above the houses of the dead's relatives.[83] This brings to mind the Taíno creation story, where Yayael's bones were placed in a gourd, only to be taken down and turned into the fish that would soon inhabit the sea.

Occasionally, the bodies of important people and caciques were purposefully preserved with the intention of turning them into cemís. Bodies were exhumed and dried to preserve the skin and bones, particularly the skulls, which were described by Columbus as being hung from the roofs of the Taíno houses in baskets.

The ashes of the newly deceased bones were also used by behiques in acts of endocannibalism, where the ashes would be prepared into a drink and consumed, transferring the once living spirit to the drinker.

Even in rituals that weren't associated with death, Coaybay, opias, and the presence of mortality were acknowledged. The frequent owl and bat imagery signify death, though it is noted that these effigy bowls and ritualistic tools often included representations of erect phalluses, again connecting life and fertility to death.

---

[83] "The Funerary Gourd and Bowl of the Taínos." Caney Circle. https://caneycircle.wordpress.com/ceremonies/

The Mythology of Death

There are conflicting beliefs about the part death plays in Taíno mythology, especially when it comes to the dog-like cemí, Opiyelguabirán. Some say that he stands guard over the entrance to the land of the dead, Coaybay, preventing the opias from escaping during daylight hours.

Other modern Taínos object, saying this is a conflation with the Greek mythological hellhound Cerberus. Cerberus is known for guarding the gates to the underworld, making sure the dead do not return to the land of the living.

An alternate version of Opiyelguabirán's place in Taíno mythology describes him not as a guard dog but as a guide, leading the spirits of the recently dead to their place in Coaybay.

Of course, death also takes center stage in the Taíno creation myth when Yaya kills his son, whose bones go on to become important nourishment, feeding into the idea of the cyclical nature of life. Furthermore, it is interesting to note how the Taíno associated the entrance to the underworld (the cave) with Atabey's womb where the first Taíno people emerged, demonstrating the close and cyclical relationship between life and death.[84]

In the Arawak traditions of the Carib people, who share many cultural similarities with the Taíno, there were two deities who contributed to the creation of humans. One of them was Kururumany, who was responsible for creating men, while the goddess Kulimina created women.

When Kururumany first came to earth to meet his creations, he was disappointed to find that humans were not the purely good and honest beings he'd meant them to be. As a form of punishment, Kururumany took away the gift of immortality from humans, leaving them with the inevitability of death. He also created snakes, lizards, and other reptiles.

Taíno Zombies

It isn't clear how long the belief in zombies or *zombis* existed in Taíno culture, but it can partially be explained by the melding of cultures with the enslaved Africans of the area. This sharing of belief systems is responsible for the creation of Vodou or Voodoo.

---

[84] Sague, Miguel Jr., "Further Discussions on Taíno Traditions Regarding Our Departed Loved Ones." https://www.pinterest.com/pin/further-discussions-on-taino-traditions-regarding-our-departed-loved-ones-indigenous-caribbean-network--220394975492372582/

For the early people of Haiti, zombis manifest as extremely annoying or evil people who have lost their sense of good, perhaps meaning that a body has lost its spirit altogether and been left with no conscience. As a result, the family might hire the services of a shaman to give the zombi a magic powder.

The powder, which was thought to include a powerful nerve toxin called tetrodotoxin (deadly if consumed in high enough quantities), was never used in African Vodou traditions, leading experts to believe that it was introduced by the Taíno, who were skilled at removing poisons from otherwise edible fish.

The magic powder given to the zombi would then make them appear to or actually die. Then, the body would be buried and exhumed days later. Supposedly, the surviving zombi would be under the power of the shaman who had performed the ritual, making it unable to misbehave anymore.

This "zombification" was used to subdue people with violent, criminal tendencies. Once the zombi was reanimated, they were in a catatonic state, incapable of living as they formerly had. In Vodou culture, these zombis were sometimes used as slave labor. They were shunned by their family and friends and no longer seen as containing a spirit, known as a duppy (a version of the Taíno opia).

Comparisons have been made between this poison powder drink and the 20th-century Tiki cocktail, the zombie, which was invented to dull the senses and leave the drinker in a zombie-like state.[85]

The Taíno use of poisons and toxins and the use of poisonous fish in effigy bowls and Taíno art suggests that perhaps the naturally occurring toxic substances were used by behiques in similar ways to the use of cohoba. If behiques did, in fact, ingest these substances and appear to be dead for days on end, only to reanimate later, it might suggest that the Taíno people had a tradition of zombis in their culture predating the Vodou understanding of the living dead.

There is no antidote for the pufferfish poison despite the fact that it is considered a delicacy in many parts. Haitian legend states that eating salt is the only way to return the humanity to someone who has been turned

---

[85] Physician, This Curious Life, "How to Make a Zombie." https://lifeasahuman.com/2010/mind-spirit/spirituality-and-religion/how-to-make-a-zombie/

into a zombi; otherwise, they will forever live on, acting as a slave to whoever poisoned them.[86]

Cacique Hatuey's Sacrifice

It would be impossible to discuss the relationship between the Taíno, the afterlife, and death without mentioning the legendary martyrdom of Cacique Hatuey. Hatuey was a brave chief at the time of the Spanish invasion when the Taíno people were captured, killed, enslaved, and sometimes forced to convert to Catholicism.

The tales of Spanish cruelty against the Taíno people are extremely disturbing. Accounts from the time describe babies' heads being smashed against rocks and the slicing of men in two with sharp swords.

Hatuey couldn't bear to see his people decimated like that and set about to form a resistance that even attracted the attention of some of the African slaves captured by the Spanish. Together, they developed guerilla-style fighting techniques to fight against the gunpowder and swords brandished by the Spanish.

Unable to take back his home, Hatuey and his people were forced to take to canoes and make for safety. They ended up in Cuba, where Hatuey was able to warn the other Indigenous people there that the Spanish were nearby. An attack was to be expected from the people who cared about gold above all else.

It didn't take long for the Spanish to arrive on Cuban shores, first making a settlement in what is modern Guantanamo. Hatuey and his guerilla fighters waited to make their move. Being more comfortable in the wilds of Cuba than the Spanish were, Hatuey's men managed to terrorize the Spanish for the better part of a year. They would descend from the trees and mountains with axes and macanas (similar in shape to a mace or a morning star), then disappear back where they came from, leaving the Spanish unable to follow. Hatuey was able to hold the Spanish fort under siege for three months, but forcing the colonizers off the island was another issue altogether.

After one very successful offense, the Spanish were able to capture Hatuey. They knew how difficult it would be for the Taíno to keep fighting without their cacique. He was sentenced to death. He was to be burned at the stake in February 1512.

---

[86] Allooloo, Siku, "Living Death." https://briarpatchmagazine.com/articles/view/living-death

Before his execution, though, Hatuey was urged to convert to Catholicism and leave his Taíno beliefs behind. Whether or not he was truly considering conversion before his death, what has lasted in legend since then is the question Hatuey asked his captors about their religion. He wanted to know if the Spanish would be allowed into the heaven they believed in.

The priest told him that yes, of course, the Spanish would be invited into heaven as long as they were "godly and goodly." For Hatuey, this knowledge confirmed that conversion would not be worth it. The idea of having to exist in the afterlife surrounded by the people who had destroyed his home and killed countless of his loved ones was not something he wanted. It would be better to live out his eternity in hell instead.

Chapter 8: Batey: The Ball Game and Its Mythological Significance

The word *batey* meant two things in the Taíno culture. The first meaning was simply the name of a place. The Taíno villages were called *yucayeques*. Each village layout was in the shape of a cross. There were two paths that intersected with each other. In the center of that intersection was the batey. This was the village plaza in the heart of the settlement.

In ancient Taíno culture, there were four directions on the medicine wheel: north, south, east, and west. There was also a fifth direction, and that was the axis of the entire cosmos. The batey in the intersection of the village represented the fifth direction.

The axis of the cosmos linked together the three horizontal planes of existence: the sky above, the earth, and the underworld below.

The plaza was a central meeting place for everyone in the village. It was used as a cemetery for the dead, and every communal activity took place there.

Batey the Game

Batey was the name the Taíno gave to their ball game as well. They played the game in their communal meeting spot. People were divided into two teams that consisted of between ten and thirty players.[87] Both teams would be either all men or all women; they never mixed sexes or

---

[87] Times of the Islands – Partying, Taíno -style. https://www.timespub.tc/2007/06/partying-Taíno -style/

competed against each other. The ball was crafted from tree resin or rubber from the rubber tree.

The goal of the game was to keep the ball in the air. It was never allowed to bounce more than once on the ground. To keep the ball in the air, the players could use any body part except for their hands or feet.

The Spanish observed that men and women tended to favor different body parts when keeping the ball in the air. The losing team would let the ball hit the ground for more than a single bounce.[88] The outcome of the game would determine the final decision on certain matters in the village.

Batey's Mythological Meaning

Was there any cosmological significance with either the game batey or the plaza itself? Little has been written down about these facts because the Spaniards didn't understand the importance of batey when it was played. However, archaeologists have found that many of the village plazas align with the solstices and equinoxes. The Taíno viewed the sun as the supreme creator. The rising of the three most important constellations to the Taíno also came from the east: Pleiades, Orion, and Scorpio.

The rise of the Pleiades constellation came in early June each year, which marked the start of the Taíno calendar year. Shortly after, the rains would follow, bringing the croaking frogs, leading the Taíno to believe Pleiades was the one responsible for the blessing of the rain.

The Taíno used the astrological cycles, the rising and setting of constellations seasonally across the night sky, to correlate their calendar with the climate cycle of the region. The batey helped them know which direction to look for the astrological signs in the skies. This helped the Taíno people know when to expect the rains and what seasons various birds or fish would be abundant on the island and in the waters.

Based on the astrological signs, the people determined when they needed to hold yearly rituals. The myths of the Taíno were reenacted yearly during these rituals, which for them meant time was circular and not linear. Nature continually repeated the same manifestations every year.

---

[88] Caguana Ceremonial Ball Courts Site--Historic Places in Puerto Rico and the Virgin Islands. https://www.nps.gov/nr/travel/prvi/pr25.htm

Socially, the cacique kept his position of power. He was firmly respected by the people since he appeared to predict and control the invisible forces of nature. He would tell the people when to perform the rituals and invite the seasonal rains, migratory birds, or seasonal fish to the islands.

The Maya played a similar ball game in Central America. We know a bit more about the Maya version of the game than we do about the Taíno version. For the Maya, the outcome of the game often involved human sacrifice and symbolized keeping the sun and moon floating in the sky within their orbit.

Both batey and the Maya version of the game were played with rubber balls and had similar rules. In both games, the ball wasn't allowed to roll across the ground, and players could not use their hands or feet to touch the ball. Though the Taíno were separated from the Maya and South American Arawak peoples by the Caribbean Sea, they still shared quite a few similarities in beliefs and rituals, including their ball game.[89]

The description of the celebrations of the great Taíno warrior Ornoya's defeat of an invading force led by the cacique Ornocoy shows just how important both the game of batey and the ceremonial plaza could be.

Amid dancers and the sound of drums and conch horns, Ornoya was honored by his cacique, who stopped him before he could even bow, claiming that no man of his accomplishment should bow before anyone. After the festivities, a game of batey broke out, pitting the men against the women, who, as mentioned before, never played on the same team.

Finally, the batey was also used as a place to reenact great acts of conflict and war, sometimes blurring the lines between acting and reality when true violence was inspired by the simulations, though any fighting was still a symbol of respect to Ornoya, whose name was chanted through the hills forevermore.[90]

---

[89] The Mayan Ball Game: What Exactly Was It? – History. https://www.historyonthenet.com/the-mayan-ball-game

[90] Millán, Iran, TRADITIONS & LEGENDS OF CIENFUEGOS. https://media2021.meliacuba.com/brochures/brochure-destino-cienfuegos-en-12215.pdf

Chapter 9: The Enduring Legacy of Taíno Mythology

While the textbooks claim that the Taíno were driven to extinction after Christopher Columbus first made contact and the Spanish systematically decimated their population, Taíno traditions live on to this day, daring us to rethink our definition of "extinct."

There's a growing community of people with Caribbean and Taíno heritage all over the world discovering their roots and finding out more about the culture that so many believed to be a thing of the past. It can be challenging for descendants of the original Taíno to trace back their heritage, especially considering the lack of information on the culture. In Western schools, many are taught about how Columbus made contact with the Maya people, but rarely is anything mentioned about the Taíno, though they were, in fact, the first people in the New World Columbus met.

That being said, the notion that the Taíno people disappeared for centuries and are now reappearing is incorrect. The idea that all the Taíno were killed has been referred to as a "paper genocide," which references how the Spanish classified the Indigenous populations after the Taíno slaves were freed in 1533. Any Spaniard who wanted to keep their slave had only to reclassify them as African, throwing the records off forever.

By 1802, there were no "Indians" documented at all in the Puerto Rican census, hence the idea of the Taíno appearing extinct on paper. In

Cuba, the revolution took a big toll on the surviving Taíno population, as the government reinforced the idea of Taíno extinction in an attempt to diminish the racial differences in the population and instead promote a unified "Cuban" identity.

The Taíno were never completely extinguished, which is why we still have a connection to their customs and traditions now. After the Spanish colonized the Caribbean, many Taíno fled to live in the mountains, where they still exist to this day in regions of Cuba and the Dominican Republic.

In Puerto Rico, the Taíno used similar tactics to survive, but Project Bootstrap in the 1940s forced many of the Indigenous population into more urban settings. Many left Puerto Rico altogether, hopeful to find greener pastures elsewhere. For the Taíno who stayed, their culture started to be shared more with urban populations, starting a revival of Taíno traditions that truly took off in the 1970s and grew stronger toward the end of the 20th century.

The year 2003 was another key turning point for the Taíno of Puerto Rico when a study was done on the DNA of the population. The results showed that 61.1 percent of those studied had Indigenous mitochondrial DNA. Local school groups started incorporating the teaching of the Taíno language and history, while activist groups began working to gain official recognition from the government and preserve tribal sites still in existence.

In Cuba, the recognition of the Taíno culture took a different journey. Similarly to other Caribbean areas, the Taíno who survived the Spanish occupation were eventually driven to the hills. After the collapse of the Soviet Union in 1991, the country faced a serious scarcity of both food and medicine, and the government was forced to use ancient Indigenous knowledge.

Modern Cuba is known for its healthcare system and medical discoveries. In fact, it wasn't until researchers turned to Indigenous knowledge that they discovered the potential of scorpion poison as a cancer treatment.[91] The Taíno used the venom to treat arthritis, so the anti-inflammatory properties of the poison may have the capability to

---

[91] Catarina Rapôso. Scorpion and spider venoms in cancer treatment: state of the art, challenges, and perspectives - https://pmc.ncbi.nlm.nih.gov/articles/PMC6410669/#:~:text=It%20is%20clear%20that%20scorpion,%2C%20and%2For%20ion%20channels

shrink tumors.[92] At this time, there is limited evidence to prove its effectiveness.

In Jamaica, the modern-day population has primarily African heritage, but the country still recognizes its Taíno history. Even the Jamaican coat of arms features two Taíno people, a man and a woman, standing on either side of a shield with five pineapples. The Jamaican multicultural identity is further displayed in their motto, which is displayed across the bottom of the coat of arms: "Out of Many, One People."[93]

Given the multicultural nature of the Caribbean and the West Indies, many are opposed to trying to carve out a separate identity for the Taíno, while others say that anyone seeking that status is merely after government subsidies or land grants. There are still unfortunate stereotypes of those who identify the Taíno as uneducated country folk.

Taíno Practices Today

Despite the politics, there are many who carry on the traditions of the Taíno, including the knowledge of gardening and medicinal healing. There are also those who pray to the sun and moon for good weather and use the lunar cycles to inform planting and harvesting practices. The strategies the Taíno had for building weather-resistant homes are still practiced today. For communities with limited resources, the Taíno farming style has kept generations thriving.

This can also be seen in the way Taíno communities prepare their food, using ancient knowledge to properly remove the poison from certain fish and how to prepare the yucca flour so that it can be preserved for long periods of time and be used to bake cassava bread. The old Taíno way of shredding yucca against grated stone has been updated into the *guayo,* and in Cuba, you can still get rice and beans served in coconut shells, just as the Taíno once did.

---

[92] Cuba's Taíno People: A Flourishing Culture, Believed Extinct. https://www.bbc.com/travel/article/20190205-cubas-tano-people-a-flourishing-culture-believed-extinct

[93] Haile, Shenhat. "Investigating Discourses of Indigeneity and Taíno Survival in Jamaica."

Taíno women preparing cassava bread.[vi]

Outside of the Caribbean, there are many groups in the United States working to raise awareness of and support for the Taíno culture. The Caney Indian Spiritual Circle was established in 1982 in Pittsburg, Pennsylvania, and since then, they have been providing education on Taíno beliefs, as well as performing traditional ceremonies and tribal dances in the area.

The Indigenous Caribbean Network is an online platform with plenty of information on Taíno traditions and offers space for contributors to start conversations and ask questions. In 1998, the United Federation of Taíno People was formed "to promote the self-determination and protection of the human rights, culture, traditions, and sacred lands of Taíno and other Caribbean Indigenous Peoples." The federation has since worked closely with the United Nations to safeguard and revitalize the Taíno traditions.

While there are several organizations working to reestablish the knowledge of the Taíno language, there are several words that have lasted through the centuries and are still in common use today. "Hammock," "barbeque," "manatee," "canoe," "tobacco," "iguana," and "hurricane" are all words we can trace back to the original Taíno people and were then adopted by the Spanish.

In 2024, an exhibit ran at the National Museum of Puerto Rican Arts & Culture and the African American Cultural Center and Museum of Florida entitled "Caribbean Indigenous Resistance." Part of the exhibit looked at the lasting Taíno practices in culture and technology, including how Taíno symbols are still frequently used in tattoo designs. The exhibit also explored the use of hammocks (a Taíno invention) on lunar missions, starting with Apollo 13.

Many of the traditional Taíno artistic practices have lived on as well, both in music and craftwork. Weaving remains an important custom, as well as the act of making instruments and canoes out of logs. In many classrooms across North America, maracas are a common percussion instrument, though few know where they originated from.[94] It is believed the Taíno used a form of maracas, so it is possible they might have originated with the Taíno people.

Lasting Legends

While many of the Taíno myths live on today in both written and oral history, the stories of real Taíno men and women have since been turned into legends that persist in our imagination, including perhaps the only two Taíno queens.

Loiza, a town in Puerto Rico, is supposedly named after a female cacique of the same name. When the Spanish invaded, many Taíno women were forced to wed the Spaniards just to secure their survival, but for Loiza, it was true love that led her to the conquistador Pedro Mejias. Believing this to be a complete betrayal of her people, especially when the Spanish were responsible for so many Taíno deaths, several other caciques gathered together and planned to assassinate Loiza.

Other stories tell of even more betrayals on Loiza's part, including converting to Catholicism and changing her name to the Spanish "Luisa," though it is reasonable to assume she was merely protecting her

---

[94] Puerto Rican Cultural Center - Music, Dance, and Culture of Puerto Rico. https://www.prfdance.org/taino.history.ALL.htm

life. Despite her ruthless murder and tarnished reputation, Loíza's memory lives on, as many consider her to be a symbol of multiculturalism in the town to this day, as the man she fell in love with was not only Spanish but also African.

In 1972, an artist by the name of Lolita Cuevas visited the town of Loíza. When she was there, she was supposedly visited in the night by the spirit of the Taíno cacique Loíza, and she immediately got to painting when she awoke. She worked through the night, and the painting that came out of the ghostly visit is still hanging in the Loíza town hall to this day.[95]

Another Taíno queen whose story lives on is that of Anacaona, the cacique hailing from Haiti. She was from a family of caciques, inheriting her brother's rule after his death, but she was also married to a great cacique known as Caonabo.

Legend has it that when the Spanish arrived, they pretended to honor Caonabo with gifts, including silver handcuffs they swore were worn by great men during prestigious ceremonies. Worried (and rightly so) that Caonabo would be able to inspire a revolt against the Spanish, Columbus himself ordered Caonabo's arrest and subsequent execution in Spain.

After her husband was killed in a shipwreck on his way to Europe, Anacaona inherited his cacicazgo, which she ruled in conjunction with the Spanish in relative peace, paying them taxes in the form of food and gold. Eventually, the Spanish grew threatened by the people's love of Anacaona and worried that she, too, would raise enough support to overthrow them.

Anacaona was arrested after welcoming a visit from the Spanish, who burned her chiefs alive while she was hanged outside. Her legacy lives on in the Anacaona cave system in Haiti, where she was supposedly born. It is seen as a mystical place for visitors now.

A book in the *Royal Diaries* series (beloved by young female audiences) has been written featuring Anacaona, imagining what she might have written in a journal during her youth.[96]

---

[95] "Loíza: The Heart of Puerto Rico's Black Culture."
https://blackvoicenews.com/2018/04/01/loiza-the-heart-of-puerto-ricos-black-culture/
[96] "Anacaona." Infinite Women. https://www.infinite-women.com/women/anacaona/

Enduring Mythology

There are ways of telling time without clocks or watches. When the lizards descend from the palm trees for water, that's a good indication that the sun is high in the sky.

The way modern Taíno interact with the natural world very much lines up with how Columbus and his men wrote about the people they met in Puerto Rico. There is a respect for what the earth provides and a deep spiritual feeling that the trees, plants, and animals must be thanked for what humans take from them.[97]

The Taíno creation myth is likely the most well known of the Taíno legends, and there are several ways that the lessons and themes in that tale are still honored today. Environmental stewardship, inspired by the way Atabey created the natural world, is still vital to the Taíno belief system.

We know that the Taíno used gourds for many reasons, both practical and spiritual. Yaya kept the bones of his son in a gourd. These bones were later turned into the fish that now fill the ocean. Today, gourds are decorated all over the Americas, a tradition that some say might have been started by the Taíno.

The conch or *guamo* still plays an important ceremonial role in Taíno culture, just as it did hundreds of years ago. The shells were used to signal the beginning of a ritual or ceremony. The first Spanish who met the Taíno noted that most of the population carried a shell with them to be used as a trumpet to communicate. There are still graves surrounded by conch shells in modern-day Cuba. These are meant to keep away evil spirits in conjunction with thatch.[98]

There are several myths and stories of Taíno folklore that have survived the centuries, but one of the most commonly told stories that was published in an illustrated children's book is the tale of how Puerto Rico became an island. This is *The Golden Flower* by Nina Jaffe.

In the myth, Puerto Rico was no more than a treeless mountain in a desert. A young boy finds all kinds of seeds and saves them, eventually planting them at the top of the mountain. Later, the seeds grow into a

---

[97] Poole, Robert. "Who Were the Taíno, the Original Inhabitants of Columbus' Island Colonies?" https://www.smithsonianmag.com/history/who-were-taino-original-inhabitants-columbus-island-73824867/

[98] Rodriguez, William. Spirals from the Past- Sea Shell Trumpets. https://www.archaicroots.com/education/spirals-from-the-past-shell-trumpets/

great forest. When the people notice the forest, they go exploring and find a big golden blossom. Soon, the flower turns into a giant, shining globe.

Each wants to keep the golden orb for themselves. Two men start fighting over it, only to discover that it is, in fact, a pumpkin. The fight tore the pumpkin off the stem, and it went rolling down the mountain, cracking open on the way down. To everyone's surprise, a flood of water poured out of the pumpkin, surrounding the mountain with plentiful ocean life and turning Puerto Rico into the island we know it to be today.[99]

Today, tourism plays a big part in the continuance of Taíno traditions, bringing awareness and funding to activism efforts. Los Haitises National Park in the Dominican Republic is the perfect place to see where Taíno practices were founded and the cave paintings of giant birds swooping down and cemís deserving of worship.

Hotels and resorts in the Caribbean also make use of the Taíno arts to entertain their guests, sharing dances and storytelling that shed light on the history of the land and educate tourists on the mythology and religion of the original peoples.[100]

---

[99] Jaffe, Nina, "The Golden Flower."
[100] Wittgreen. "Matum Show in Punta Cana." https://bpprivilegeclub.com/blog/matum-show-in-punta-cana/

Conclusion

The enduring legacy of the Taíno culture, religion, and mythology is remarkable for many reasons, especially considering the long-accepted theory that they were rendered completely extinct by the conquering Spanish.

From language to storytelling, from farming to culinary techniques, the Taíno traditions have stuck with us since the Arawak people (which the Taíno are a subgroup of) first came to the Antilles in 400 BCE. Whenever we barbeque, swing in a hammock, or take a canoe ride, it is the Taíno we have to thank.

In terms of mythology, the creation stories of the Taíno demonstrate the importance of nature and the elements, evidenced by the multiple tales covering how the ocean came to be filled with fish. All the overlapping myths of Yaya and the four sons of Itiba Cahubaba feature pieces of the natural world, including animals and plants, such as gourds.

Animals frequently appear in Taíno mythology, both as cemís or gods, like the woodpecker Inriri, or as food sources that also deserve honor, such as the iguana. Many animals appear as characters in Taíno myths and folklore, like the owl, who earned his own story to explain how he became nocturnal. The Taíno were also known to keep animals as domesticated pets (like parrots and dogs) while farming and keeping other animals for nourishment, like the hutia.

The effects of the Europeans' forceful and violent colonization of the Caribbean have stripped us of a clear knowledge of Taíno culture, often leaving future generations with only the colonizers' accounts of the local traditions to learn from. The meaning and purpose of batey, both as a game and as a ceremonial space, were not completely understood by the Spanish, leaving an incomplete history behind them.

Despite Spanish efforts to eradicate the Taíno, the traditions live on with the people of the Caribbean, as seen in the way the Neo-Taíno movement has picked up the mantle, starting a resurgence of the culture all over South and North America.

Though the Taíno were often sent fleeing to the hills to escape plague and violence, others assimilated into the invading population, ensuring that the stories and rituals survived generations. The creation of the Vodou or Voodoo religion also has the Taíno religion to thank as one of its contributing sources, particularly to the Haitian form of the religion.

The mermaids and sea monsters of Taíno mythology have held tightly in our collective imagination as well. To this day, visitors can go see Taíno pictographs and cave paintings all over Puerto Rico and the Caribbean. Novelizations such as Monique Roffey's *The Mermaid of Black Conch* offer us a window into how Taíno culture is interpreted by modern audiences. Everyone is encouraged to enjoy the music and dances of the ancient Taíno still being performed to this day.

Taíno cave pictographs.[vii]

Glossary

- Achiano - Star of the South
- Atabey - Mother goddess
- Barbacoa or barabicu - Barbeque
- Batey - Ball game and plaza where the Taíno conducted ceremonies, rituals, and held gatherings
- Bayamanaco - The old man who appears in the Turtle Woman creation myth, teaching a lasting lesson to Deminán and his brothers.
- Bohios - Taíno houses, which were built low to the ground with thatched roofs to withstand the effects of great storms
- Behiques - The shamans, religious leaders, and medicine men of Taíno culture
- Boinayel - God of the sun
- Borikén - The present-day island of Puerto Rico
- Caciques - The Taíno leaders
- Cacicazgo - A chiefdom
- Caracaracol - People afflicted with scars or scabby skin
- Casabe - Bread made from yucca flour
- Cemí or zemi - Sculptural iterations of Taíno gods and goddesses

- Ciboney - Taíno people of Jamaica and central Cuba
- Coaybay - The Taíno underworld or land of the dead
- Cohoba - A hallucinogen made from the ground seeds of the *Anadenanthera peregrina* tree
- Colibri - Hummingbird
- Deminán - One of the quadruplets born to Itiba Cahubaba (a form of Atabey) responsible for breaking Yaya's gourd and filling the oceans with his tears
- Duhos - Ceremonial seats for caciques or behiques
- Goeiza - Spirits of the living
- Guabancex - Goddess of storms and destruction and a manifestation of Atabey
- Guacar - Brother of Yúcahu, who transforms himself into Juracán
- Guaiko - The Taíno medicine wheel
- Guamo – Conch
- Guanaho - Turkey
- Guani - Bee hummingbird
- Guaraguao - Hawk
- Hamaka – Hammock
- Huracán - Hurricane
- Hutia - Capybara-like rodents farmed for eating
- Itiba Cahubaba - Another form of the goddess Atabey
- Iwana - Iguana
- Jicotea - Tortoise
- Juracán - Son of Atabey, twin brother of Yúcahu, and the god of storms
- Karaya - Spirit of the moon and the Taíno word for moon
- Kahaya - Shark
- Kaiman - Crocodile
- Koromo - Star of the West

- Ku - Middle realm of the spirit world, or Earth
- Locuo - The first man
- Maboyas - Evil spirits
- Maquetaurie Guayaba - God of the underworld
- Maroya - God of the moon
- Múcaro - Owl
- Naborias - Commoners in Taíno society
- Nitaínos - Taíno nobility
- Opia or hupia - Spirits of the dead
- Querequete - Nighthawk
- Rakuno - Star of the North
- Sobaiko - Star of the East
- Turey - Upper realm of the spirit world
- Yaboa - Night heron
- Yaya - Creator god
- Yúcahu - Spirit of masculine fertility
- Yucayeques - Taíno villages
- Yucca - Nourishing plant root, like tapioca
- Zombis - West African or Vodou interpretation of zombies

Here's another book by Enthralling History that you might like

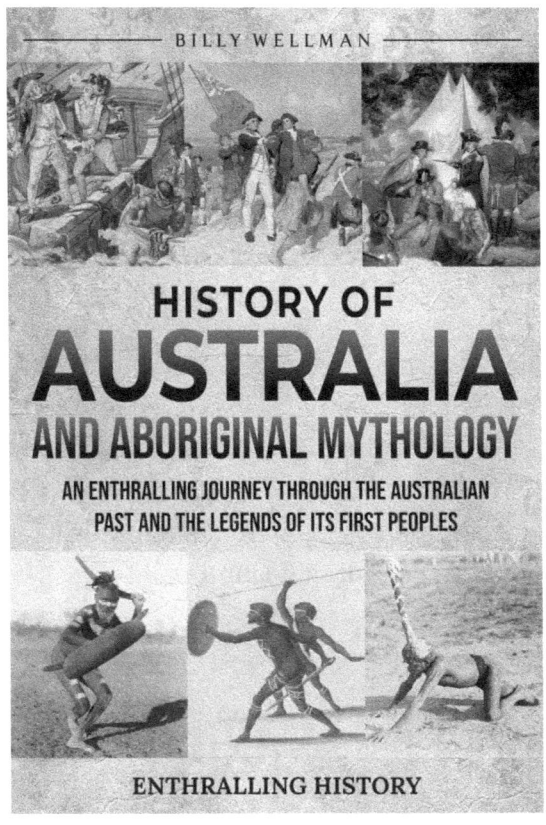

Free limited time bonus

Stop for a moment. We have a free bonus set up for you. The problem is this: we forget 90% of everything that we read after 7 days. Crazy fact, right? Here's the solution: we've created a printable, 1-page pdf summary for this book that you're reading now. All you have to do to get your free pdf summary is to go to the following website:
https://livetolearn.lpages.co/enthrallinghistory/

Or, Scan the QR code!

Bibliography

"Anacaona." Infinite Women, https://www.infinite-women.com/women/anacaona/. Accessed 15 Mar. 2024.

A New Step Forward in the Future Recovery of the Puerto Rican Parrot | U.S. Fish & Wildlife Service. 3 Mar. 2022, https://www.fws.gov/press-release/2022-03/new-step-forward-future-recovery-puerto-rican-parrot.

Allooloo, Siku, "Living Death," Feb. 8, 2016, https://briarpatchmagazine.com/articles/view/living-death. Accessed 15 Mar. 2024.

Atkinson, Leslie Gail, "The Earliest Inhabitants: The Dynamics of the Jamaican Taíno." University of the West Indies Press, 2006.

"Cemi and Headdress," www.unionhiwayawa.com, http://www.unionhiwayawa.com/444656547. Accessed 15 Mar. 2024.

"Chapter 1. Storms and Gods in a Spanish Sea." *Sea of Storms: A History of Hurricanes in the Greater Caribbean from Columbus to Katrina*, Princeton: Princeton University Press, 2016, pp. 1-32. https://doi.org/10.1515/9781400852086-003

Ciguapa – Mythical Creatures Guide. https://www.mythicalcreaturesguide.com/ciguapa/. Accessed 15 Mar. 2024.

Coat of Arms – Jamaica Information Service. https://jis.gov.jm/information/symbols/jamaican-coat-of-arms/. Accessed 15 Mar. 2024.

"Coqui – Encantada: Isle of Myths." ENCANTADA Isle of Myths, mitosencantado.com/coqui/. Accessed 15 Mar. 2024.

Cuba's Taíno People: A Flourishing Culture, Believed Extinct. https://www.bbc.com/travel/article/20190205-cubas-tano-people-a-flourishing-culture-believed-extinct. Accessed 15 Mar. 2024.

Didymus, John Thomas. "Lusca." Fairy Tales and Myths, 7 Dec. 2023, https://www.fairytalesandmyths.com/lusca/.

Doyle, James A., "Arte del Mar," Metropolitan Museum of Art Bulletin, Art of Early Caribbean, Winter 2020

Dubois, Laurent. Haiti Reader: History, Culture, Politics. Duke University Press, 2020.

"El Yunque: Its History." El Yunque Inns, www.elyunqueinns.com/el-yunque-its-history. Accessed 15 Mar. 2024.

Farabee, William Curtis. The Central Arawaks. Cambridge University Press, 2009.

"The Funerary Gourd and Bowl of the Taínos." Caney Circle, 21 Feb. 2016, https://caneycircle.wordpress.com/guordandbowlburial/.

Gilad, Elon. "A Thanksgiving Riddle: Why Are Turkeys Called Turkeys?" Haaretz, 23 Nov. 2015. Haaretz, https://www.haaretz.com/archaeology/2015-11-23/ty-article/.premium/why-are-turkeys-called-turkeys/0000017f-e29a-d804-ad7f-f3fa3b780000.

Gorman, Gerard, "Woodpeckers of the World," Buffalo (New York): Firefly Books, The Quarterly Review of Biology, vol. 91, no. 2, June 2016, pp. 230-230.

Guitar, Lynne, "Documenting the Myth of Taíno Extinction," Journal of Caribbean Amerindian History and Anthropology, January 2002.

Haile, Shenhat. "Investigating Discourses of Indigeneity and Taíno Survival in Jamaica." Caribbean Quilt, vol. 6, no. 1, Feb. 2022, pp. 26-35. DOI.org (Crossref), https://doi.org/10.33137/cq.v6i1.35960.

Ihearthula. "Folktale Friday: Lusca and the Blue Holes." 26 Mar. 2021, https://ihearthula.com/2021/03/26/folktale-friday-lusca-and-the-blue-holes/.

"Indigenous Caribbean Network." Tradition of the Male Harsh Menstruation Spirit. Indigenous Caribbean Network, indigenouscaribbean.ning.com/m/blogpost?id=2030313%3ABlogPost%3A67964. Accessed 15 Mar. 2024.

History of the Taíno Indians. http://www.fjcollazo.com/documents/TanioIndRpt.htm. Accessed 15 Mar. 2024

"How the History of Caribbean Barbecue Produced the Spicy, Fruity Flavors We Know Today." Food & Wine, https://www.foodandwine.com/cradle-of-barbecue-7550634.

"Human and Hutia (Isolobodon Portoricensis) Interactions in Pre-Columbian Hispaniola: The Isotopic and Morphological Evidence - ScienceDirect." ScienceDirect.Com | Science, Health and Medical Journals, Full Text Articles and Books., https://www.sciencedirect.com/science/article/pii/S2352409X21001255. Accessed 15 Mar. 2024.

Isbani, Eli, "Notes on the Taíno Language," Taíno Language, Sept. 23, 2011, https://Taínolanguage.wordpress.com/2011/09/23/the-morpheme-of-k/

Jaffe, Nina, "The Golden Flower," Simon & Schuster Books for Young Readers, 1996.

"J. Lo's 'This Is Me...Now: A Love Story': Is the Hummingbird Legend Real? A Historian Weighs In." TODAY.Com, 16 Feb. 2024, https://www.today.com/popculture/jennifer-lopez-hummingbird-legend-this-is-me-now-rcna138695.

Keegan, William F. Taíno Indian Myth and Practice: The Arrival of the Stranger King. University Press of Florida, 2007.

Keegan, William F., and Lisabeth A. Carlson. Talking Taíno: Essays on Caribbean Natural History from a Native Perspective. University of Alabama Press, 2008.

La India Maldita en tradiciones y leyendas de Cienfuegos | Cuba. 15 Jan. 2024, https://cubamemorias.com/la-india-maldita-en-tradiciones-y-leyendas-de-cienfuegos/.

"Loíza: The Heart of Puerto Rico's Black Culture." Hudson Valley Press, 18 Apr. 2018, https://hudsonvalleypress.com/2018/04/18/loiza-the-heart-of-puerto-ricos-black-culture/.

López, Ivan Rodríguez, "Antillean Islander Space: On the Religious Beliefs and Representations of the Taíno People," Journal of Religious History, Feb. 2016.

Miate, Liana. "Eris." World History Encyclopedia, https://www.worldhistory.org/Eris/. Accessed 15 Mar. 2024

Millán, Iran, TRADITIONS & LEGENDS OF CIENFUEGOS, Melia Hotels International, https://media2021.meliacuba.com/brochures/brochure-destino-cienfuegos-en-12215.pdf

Mikkola, Heimo, editor. Bats - Disease-Prone but Beneficial. IntechOpen, 2022. DOI.org (Crossref), https://doi.org/10.5772/intechopen.95729.

Muir, Evie. "Black Mermaid Folklore Has Been Around Long Before Disney's The Little Mermaid," https://www.refinery29.com/en-us/black-mermaids-ariel-history. Accessed 15 Mar. 2024.

Oliver, José R. Caciques and Cemí Idols: The Web Spun by Taíno Rulers between Hispaniola and Puerto Rico. University of Alabama Press, 2009.

Paralitici, Carlos, "Myth of Creation (Taíno Mythology)," West Side Destination.com, May 5th, 2020, https://wsdestination.com/2020/05/05/myth-of-creation-Taíno-mythology/

Pethick, Kris. "Myths Legends And Superstitions Of Puerto Rico." Culture Trip, The Culture Trip, 14 Mar. 2018, https://theculturetrip.com/caribbean/puerto-rico/articles/10-myths-legends-and-superstitions-of-puerto-rico.

Physician, This Curious Life, "How to Make a Zombie" – LIFE AS A HUMAN. 23 Apr. 2010, https://lifeasahuman.com/2010/mind-spirit/spirituality-and-religion/how-to-make-a-zombie/.

Poole, Robert. "Who Were the Taíno, the Original Inhabitants of Columbus' Island Colonies?" Smithsonian.Com, Smithsonian Institution, www.smithsonianmag.com/history/who-were-Taíno-original-inhabitants-columbus-island-73824867/. Accessed 15 Mar. 2024.

Poviones-Bishop, Maria, "The Bat and The Guava - Life and Death in The Taíno Worldview," Kislak Family Foundation, July 30th, 2001.

Puerto Rican Cultural Center - Music, Dance, and Culture of Puerto Rico. https://www.prfdance.org/Taíno.history.ALL.htm. Accessed 15 Mar. 2024

R., Adam. "The Legend of Coqui and the Goddess." Vamos Rincon, 14 Sept. 2021, vamosrincon.com/history-and-culture/the-legend-of-coqui-and-the-goddess/.

"Rare Taíno Stone Ceremonial Axe Owl Form" Artemis Gallery, Dec 2, 2021, https://www.bidsquare.com/online-auctions/artemis-gallery/rare-Ta%C3%ADno%20-stone-ceremonial-axe-owl-form-2533380

Rodriguez, William. Spirals from the Past- Sea Shell Trumpets - Archaic Roots - Education. 17 Jan. 2020, https://www.archaicroots.com/education/spirals-from-the-past-shell-trumpets/.

"The Royal Diaries: Anacaona, Golden Flower." Historical Novel Society, https://historicalnovelsociety.org/reviews/the-royal-diaries-anacaona-golden-flower/. Accessed 15 Mar. 2024.

Sagué-Machiran, Miguel A., "Canoa: Taíno Indigenous Dream River Journey," iUniverse, March 18, 2016.

Sague, Miguel Jr., "Further Discussions on Taíno Traditions Regarding Our Departed Loved Ones," October 9, 2012, https://indigenouscaribbean.ning.com/profiles/blogs/further-discussions-on-Taíno-traditions-regarding-our-departed-lo. Accessed 15 Mar. 2024

Sague, Miguel Jr, "Turkeys in the Caribbean," October 13, 2022, https://indigenouscaribbean.ning.com/profiles/blogs/turkeys-in-the-caribbean. Accessed 15 Mar. 2024.

Sague, Miguel Jr., "Jaguars in the Caribbean?" February 23, 2009, https://indigenouscaribbean.ning.com/profiles/blogs/jaguars-in-the-caribbean. Accessed 15 Mar. 2024.

Sague, Miguel Jr., "The Identity of GuaBanCex, Spirit of Natural Disasters," July 26, 2014 https://indigenouscaribbean.ning.com/profiles/blogs/the-identity-of-guabancex-spirit-of-natural-disasters. Accessed 15 Mar. 2024.

SEVEN SIRIK SEEDING CEREMONY, Caney Circle, https://www.caneycircle.org/docs/10-ceremony-seven-sirik-seeding-ceremony/. Accessed 15 Mar. 2024.

Socotra, Vic, "The Goddess of Storms," https://www.vicsocotra.com/wordpress/2016/06/13144/. Accessed 15 Mar. 2024.

"Taíno Zemís and Duhos (Article) | Taíno." Khan Academy, https://www.khanacademy.org/humanities/art-americas/early-cultures/xf20f462f:Taíno/a/Taíno-zemis-and-duhos.

Taíno | History & Culture | Britannica. 10 Mar. 2024, https://www.britannica.com/topic/Taíno.

"Taíno Society." Historical Archaeology, www.floridamuseum.ufl.edu/histarch/research/haiti/en-bas-saline/Taíno-society/. Accessed 15 Mar. 2024.

"The Taíno Myth of the Cursed Creator - Bill Keegan." TED, TED-Ed, ed.ted.com/lessons/the-Ta%C3%ADno-myth-of-the-cursed-creator-bill-keegan. Accessed 15 Mar. 2024.

"Thor." Norse Mythology for Smart People, https://norse-mythology.org/gods-and-creatures/the-aesir-gods-and-goddesses/thor/. Accessed 15 Mar. 2024.

Times of the Islands – Mother Sea Turtle. https://www.timespub.tc/2008/04/mother-sea-turtle/. Accessed 15 Mar. 2024.

"Tribes - Native Voices." U.S. National Library of Medicine, National Institutes of Health, www.nlm.nih.gov/nativevoices/timeline/170.html#:~:text=Christopher%20Columbus%2C%20who%20needs%20to,culture%20on%20Hispaniola%20is%20gone. Accessed 15 Mar. 2024.

Vínculo, Obtener, et al. La Ciguapa – The Woman with Backwards Feet. https://www.artisticord.com/2013/09/la-ciguapa-dominican-succubus.html. Accessed 15 Mar. 2024.

Wagschal, Steven. Minding Animals In The Old And New Worlds: A Cognitive Historical Analysis. University Of Toronto Press, 2018.

"Webster's Dictionary 1828 - Alco." Websters Dictionary 1828, webstersdictionary1828.com/Dictionary/alco. Accessed 15 Mar. 2024.

Wildlife, Defenders of. "El Yunque National Forest and the Puerto Rican Parrot: A Story of Peril and Perseverance." *Wild Without End*, 3 Nov. 2021, https://medium.com/wild-without-end/el-yunque-national-forest-and-the-puerto-rican-parrot-a-story-of-peril-and-perseverance-d3a37a07fcf2

Wittgreen. "Matum Show in Punta Cana," Privilege Club - #VacationAsYouAre. *The Blog - Privilege Club* ~ 27 Feb. 2024, https://bpprivilegeclub.com/blog/matum-show-in-punta-cana/.

Image Sources

i https://commons.wikimedia.org/wiki/File:Bird_figure_taino.jpg

ii National Museum of the American Indian, Smithsonian Institution, CC BY-SA 4.0 <https://creativecommons.org/licenses/by-sa/4.0>, via Wikimedia Commons, https://commons.wikimedia.org/wiki/File:Demin%C3%A1n_Caracaracol.jpg

iii https://commons.wikimedia.org/wiki/File:Cohoba_inhaler.jpg

iv https://commons.wikimedia.org/wiki/File:Duho_stool.jpg

v Gift of Brian and Florence Mahony, CC0, via Wikimedia Commons https://commons.wikimedia.org/wiki/File:Spatula,_900%E2%80%931492._Caribbean,_Greater_Antilles,_Taino,_10th-15th_century._Manatee_bone.jpg

vi https://commons.wikimedia.org/wiki/File:Ta%C3%ADno_women_preparing_cassava_bread.png

vii Danu Widjajanto, CC BY-SA 4.0 <https://creativecommons.org/licenses/by-sa/4.0>, via Wikimedia Commons, https://commons.wikimedia.org/wiki/File:Ta%C3%ADno_pictographs_Cuevas_de_las_Maravillas.jpg

www.ingramcontent.com/pod-product-compliance
Lightning Source LLC
Chambersburg PA
CBHW070340010526
44107CB00004B/565